Teen Rights
At Home, At School, Online

Kathiann M. Kowalski

Enslow Publishers, Inc.

40 Industrial Road	PO Box 38
Box 398	Aldershot
Berkeley Heights, NJ 07922	Hants GU12 6BP
USA	UK

http://www.enslow.com

This book is dedicated to my daughter, Bethany Meissner.

Library of Congress Cataloging-in-Publication Data

Kowalski, Kathiann M., 1955–
    Teen rights : at home, at school, online / Kathiann M. Kowalski
        p. cm. — (Issues in focus)
    Includes bibliographical references and index.
    Summary: Discusses the legal rights of teenagers in a variety of
situations, such as health care decisions, school drug testing and discrimination, and using the Internet, and cites examples of court
cases that deal with these issues.
    ISBN 0-7660-1242-5
    1. Teenagers—Civil rights—United States—Juvenile literature.
    2. Children's rights—United States—Juvenile literature.
    [1. Teenagers—Legal status, laws, etc. 2. Children's rights. 3. Law.]
    I. Title. II. Issues in focus (Hillside, N.J.)
    HQ796.K683 2000
    305.235'0973—dc21
                          99-043565

Printed in the United States of America

10 9 8 7 6 5 4 3

To Our Readers:
All Internet addresses in this book were active and appropriate when we
went to press. Any comments or suggestions can be sent by e-mail to
comments@enslow.com or to the address on the back cover.

Illustration Credits: © Corel Corporation, p. 10; Photos by
Kathiann M. Kowalski, pp. 12, 17, 29, 33, 51, 53, 62, 64, 68,
78, 84, 92, 98, 102; Photo by Tom Moore, p. 89.

Cover Illustration: Photo by Kathiann M. Kowalski.

Contents

Acknowledgments

The author gratefully acknowledges the assistance and insights she received from the following people and groups: American Civil Liberties Union; Ariel Albores; Jane Blackie; Tim Chatlos; Harriet Davis; Abigail English; Jennifer Gerres; Jennifer Kirallah; Knox County Teen Court; Daniel and Amy Kowalski; Jessica McNally; Katelyn Melton; Steven C. Miles, Analtech Inc.; Tom Moore; Anna Moser; National Crime Prevention Council; Vicky Petryshyn; Anne and Christopher Safrath; Wendy Williams; Steve Wilgus; Chris, Laura, and Bethany Meissner; and Mike Meissner.

1

Everyone Has Rights—Right?

Dominique Moceanu was a winner. At age fourteen she won a spot on the United States Olympic women's gymnastics team. Then Dominique and her teammates gave great performances at the 1996 Olympics. Their efforts paid off. Dominique and her teammates brought home gold medals.

Dominique's gold medal came after years of hard work. Training meant Dominique sometimes gave up trips to the mall. At times, she practiced instead of riding her bike. Sometimes she even gave up playing with her sister, Christina. But Dominique loved gymnastics.[1]

"And my parents were the best," she

said in her autobiography. "They supported me strongly and encouraged me every way they could."[2]

Two years later, things changed. In 1998 seventeen-year-old Dominique telephoned her parents. She was not coming home. "Next time you hear from me," Dominique said, "it will be from a lawyer."[3]

In fall 1998 Dominique filed a lawsuit in Houston, Texas. She had earned over $1 million as a gymnast. But she could not control that money. Until Dominique turned thirty-five, her parents controlled her funds. Now Dominique claimed that her father, Dumitru Moceanu, squandered her earnings.

Dominique wanted the court to emancipate her.[4] Emancipation makes a child a legal adult. It frees a child from parental control. At the same time, it excuses parents from any further duties.

Dominique's lawyers said that Dominique should control her own life. Dominique wanted to pick her own coach. She wanted to hire her own agent. She wanted to choose her own events and competitions. And she wanted to control any new income. "I feel I can handle responsibility," said Dominique.[5]

The lawsuit made national headlines. "Both parents are extremely upset," announced their lawyer, Katherine Scardino. "Their position is that she lacks the maturity to handle her own affairs."[6]

After negotiations, Dominique's parents agreed to legal emancipation. In October 1998 the Texas court ruled that Dominique was legally an adult.[7]

Five weeks later, Dominique was back in court. Now Dominique said that her father followed and harassed her.[8] She claimed that he had a violent temper.[9] On December 9, 1998, the court ordered Dominique's father to stay away from her. Otherwise, he could be arrested.[10]

In April 1999 the court lifted its order. According to Dominique's lawyer, the family settled its differences. "This has been an extremely difficult time for my family," read a statement from Dominique, "and I hope that we can now begin to move forward in support of one another."[11]

Teen Legal Issues

Issues in Dominique's legal battle with her parents affect many teens. What control do parents exert over their children? Who decides how teens must spend their time? Who controls a teen's money? What can teens do if they think their parents mistreat them?

Emancipation was one remedy the court gave Dominique. But it is rare. Most teens remain legal minors until they reach age eighteen. A minor is someone who is legally considered a child.

Outside home, young people face other issues. Can teens get medical care on their own? What rules apply if teens work? Are teens free to express themselves at school? What can schools do to discipline students? Sometimes the answers are clear. Other times, they are less clear.

All United States citizens have certain rights. These rights are stated in the United States Constitution, federal statutes, and state laws. For example, citizens have a right to freedom of speech. Citizens have the right to practice any form of religion. Citizens can also choose not to practice any religion at all.

Citizens also have the right to be free from unreasonable searches and seizures. And before the government can imprison someone or take away property, citizens have the right to due process. Due process includes steps to make sure that the government treats people fairly through the court system.

Why Treat Teens Differently?

Everyone has rights under the United States Constitution, but sometimes different rules apply to minors. Why?

United States law presumes that teens cannot make wise decisions. It assumes they lack maturity. In 1979 the Supreme Court wrote, "Most children, even in adolescence, simply are not able to make sound judgments concerning many decisions."[12]

So who makes those decisions? Often, the law defers to adults, usually the parents of the teenager. Unless it has contrary evidence, the law assumes that these adults know what is best for the teen.

Usually, parents know their children better than other adults do. Most parents care for their children. And they are legally responsible for them. Under the law, parents must provide for their children's physical and emotional well-being. As the Supreme Court explained, "The law's concept of the family rests on a presumption that parents possess what a child lacks in maturity, experience, and capacity for judgment required for making life's difficult decisions."[13]

The law also defers to schools. Schoolteachers and administrators are also supposed to have students' best interests at heart. So the law gives them control over young people's education.

Outside home and school, the law assumes that young people need protection. Child labor laws, for example, are supposed to protect young people.

During the early twentieth century, children often worked twelve hours a day in factories. A child's hand or foot could be chopped off by unsafe machinery. Fumes and exhaustion ruined many children's health.

Finally, in 1938, Congress passed a law. Congress wanted companies to stop working children to death.[14]

Statutory rape laws are also intended to protect young people. These laws make it a crime to engage in sexual activities with anyone under a certain age. That age ranges from fourteen to eighteen.[15]

Under the law, even if an underage teen or child agrees to engage in sexual activities with an adult, the adult is considered to have committed a crime. Statutory rape laws usually require the person charged to be older than the minor,[16] because lawmakers fear that adults may improperly influence a teen's sexual decisions.[17] Some lawmakers also think strict enforcement of statutory rape laws can fight high teen pregnancy rates.[18]

Some laws also focus on specific risks for young people. Statistics showed high rates for drunk driving accidents for people under age twenty-one. As a result, all states raised the legal drinking age. Now a person must be at least twenty-one years old to buy alcoholic beverages in the United States.

In summary, lawmakers have various reasons for

"Equal Justice Under Law" reads the inscription at the Supreme Court building in Washington, D.C. Nonetheless, courts may treat teens differently from adults.

treating teens differently. Sometimes they feel teens lack maturity. Sometimes they defer to parents or schools. Sometimes they feel teens need protection. Whether or not these reasons are fair, teens need to know how the law affects them.

Developing Law

It is not always easy to give a yes or no answer about the law. For one thing, laws change over time.

Two hundred years ago, hardly anyone challenged a parent's right to hit a naughty child.[19] Today, parents who hit their children hard enough to leave bruises or cause other physical injury can be charged with child abuse.[20]

Fifty years ago, children in many public schools

said prayers in class. Since then, the Supreme Court has held that school-sponsored prayers violate student rights.[21] Public schools now must respect students' religious diversity.[22]

Ten years ago, few teens were on the Internet. Since then, millions of teens have gone online. Teens use the Internet for research, entertainment, to get and send e-mail, and to chat. Now students face new issues about what is allowed online.

As times change, so does the law. Sometimes the law is spelled out in statutes. Statutes are written laws adopted by a legislature. There are both federal and state statutes.

Federal statutes apply to the whole United States. State laws often vary. Teens in Maine and Hawaii, for example, have the same rights under federal law, but their rights may be different under state law.

Other times the law develops through a number of cases on the same issue that are argued at court trials. Cases present specific facts to a court. The court applies the law to the facts and then makes a decision. This is called case law.

Interpreting cases is not always easy. Delays, appeals, and procedure questions can confuse holdings. If a court rules against a motion to dismiss, for example, that means the law allows the person bringing the lawsuit to win if he or she proves all necessary facts. It does not guarantee that the person will actually win the case.

Factual differences can produce different results. For example, although Dominique Moceanu won

Knowledge is power—teens need to know their rights in order to defend themselves legally.

emancipation, other teens may fail if they are unable to support themselves financially.

Also, there are many courts. United States Supreme Court decisions apply to the entire nation. Because of the time and effort involved, the Supreme Court can review only a limited number of cases each year. The Court chooses most cases based on whether they present a constitutional matter, or a substantial question of federal law. For practical reasons, the Court must decline review of most cases.

Meanwhile, lower courts may disagree with each other about what a federal law means. The conflict may continue until the Supreme Court finally decides to address the issue.

State court decisions can vary even more widely. Each state has its own laws. And each state has its own court system.

So, what is "the law"? The law is the body of federal, state, and local legislation, regulations, and court decisions that affects people in a particular area. This book cannot give legal advice that applies to every teen in every part of the United States. Instead, this book uses "the law" to mean general trends in federal and state law that should apply to most areas of the United States.

These trends show that teens still are treated differently from adults. In some areas, teens have more restrictions. In other areas, trends show growing protection for teen rights.

2

Teen Rights at Home

Must teens do chores? Who decides what to eat for dinner? The United States government is a democracy. But in most families, parents decide how to run their homes.

For most of America's history, family life was a legal dictatorship for young people. Parents knew what was best. Minors had to obey their parents. In almost all cases, the law would not interfere.[1]

Parental Rights and Responsibilities

Legal changes in the nineteenth century led to important protections. Until a child is

14

eighteen, parents have a legal duty to provide basic necessities. These include food, shelter, medical care, and adequate clothing. Parents must meet these needs even if it means giving up things they want for themselves.

These duties focus on "needs," not "wants." Parents cannot send a child to school without shoes. However, nothing in the law says that parents must buy designer athletic shoes for their children. Name-brand sportswear, designer jeans, and an extra dozen shirts are also luxuries.

Having these things is a privilege, not a right. Some parents will not buy them. Others make teens pay for luxuries with their allowance or part-time job wages. Either way, courts will not disagree.

The law also defers to parents on most discipline matters. Parents can ground a teen for the weekend. They can take away phone privileges. Practically no court will second-guess these decisions.

What if a teen will not do chores? Parents cannot physically force a teen to scrub floors or mow the lawn. But they can withhold privileges if teens do not help. They can ground the teen. They can refuse to lend the family car or give rides. They can refuse to pay for movie tickets or other luxuries.

In other words, teens can refuse to do chores, but parents can also refuse to grant privileges.

What about privacy? Most teens want and need privacy. Psychologists say teens should have some personal space.[2] Many parents respect their teens' privacy. But the parents usually hold the deed or lease to the home. That gives them a legal right to be in all parts of the home—even their children's rooms.

The parents' property interest also gives them legal exposure. Suppose a teen brought illegal drugs or weapons home. If those were discovered, police could potentially arrest the parents.

Beyond this, parents may worry about their children. Sudden mood swings, a drop in grades, or other changes could signal drug abuse or another problem. Talking might identify the problem. If not, parents may look for clues in their teens' rooms.

For these and other reasons, parents can lawfully search teens' rooms. This does not mean it is always the right thing to do. Indeed, experts say parents should not read a teen's diary out of pure curiosity.

Teen privacy issues at home are not legal matters. Courts generally will not interfere. Rather, privacy issues are personal matters. Teens should use communication and other personal skills to address these issues with their parents. In short, the home is not a democracy. Under the law, parents are in charge.

Parents owe children the basic necessities of life: food, clothing, and shelter. But parents have substantial say over which luxuries and privileges teens enjoy. Most courts will defer to parents' judgment. Unless abuse is an issue, the courts will not interfere.

Avoiding Abuse

Many child-rearing experts say parents should never use physical punishment. However, few child welfare agencies would prosecute parents who spank a

Phone privileges may hinge on cooperating with the rules a teen's parents set at home.

young, disobedient child on rare occasions. Sadly, some parents go far beyond this.

Child abuse is maltreatment of a child that results in injury. It can be a single incident, such as a brutal beating. Or it can be a pattern of harmful behavior, over months or years. Abuse also takes place when a parent neglects to give a child basic necessities, such as food, clothing, or shelter.

No parent has the right to abuse a child or teen. Likewise, no parent is allowed to deprive a child or teen of basic necessities. No adult is ever entitled to molest any teen or child by sexual contact.

These acts all fit under the heading of child abuse. Every state's law empowers the police, social agencies, and courts to stop child abuse.

More than one hundred twenty-five years ago, young Mary Ellen McCormick brought the problem of child abuse to the public's attention. Testifying in New York City in 1874, Mary Ellen described the horrors she endured with her adoptive parents:

> Mamma has been in the habit of whipping and beating me almost every day. She used to whip me with a twisted whip, a raw hide. The whip always left black and blue marks on my body. . . . Whenever Mamma went out I was locked up in the bedroom. . . . I have no recollection of ever being in the street in my life.[3]

Relying on a law intended to prevent people from being unlawfully imprisoned, the judge allowed social worker Etta Wheeler to bring Mary Ellen into court. Mary Ellen was removed from the home. Then the police brought criminal charges against the woman who beat her.[4]

Soon after, the New York Society for the Prevention of Cruelty to Children was organized. Its goal was to prevent child abuse.[5] Similar groups formed across the nation. Today, the Children's Defense Fund and other groups still strive to protect minors from abuse.[6]

Every state in the United States now has laws to protect children and teens. Unfortunately, child abuse is not a thing of the past. Statistics from the National Committee to Prevent Child Abuse show an alarming increase.

All child protective services agencies in the United States receive reports about alleged abuse. If all reports in 1997 were true, about 3.2 million minors were abused or neglected.[7] This number represented a 41 percent increase over 1988 reporting levels.[8] Many more abuse cases go unreported.

The National Committee to Prevent Child Abuse says abuse affects about forty-seven of every one thousand children in the United States.[9] Every minute, another six children or teens are reported abused or neglected.[10]

Why does abuse continue despite the laws against it? One problem is enforcement. Social workers do their best to investigate complaints. Yet most social workers bear heavy caseloads. They cannot always follow through immediately.

A second issue concerns policy. Many agencies aim to keep families "intact" wherever possible. They do not want to deprive a child of his or her family.

Nor do they want to punish the parents without cause. Thus, most agencies remove a child only when abuse is blatant. Sadly, this means that many children or teens remain in homes that are unsafe.[11]

Agencies are not perfect, but they can help. For this to happen, people must not keep secret what they know or suspect. Abused teens and teens who know about abusive situations can take action. They can call the police or children's welfare agency, or they can speak to a trusted adult.

Running Away

Frustrated by abuse, chemical dependency, or other difficult situations at home, many teens decide to escape. The National Children's Coalition estimates that more than one million American youths run away from home each year.[12]

Rarely do teens achieve a better life by running away. Finding food, clothing, and shelter without any income can be overwhelming. Moreover, because the runaway teen has not finished school, he or she probably cannot get a good job.

Many runaways turn to crime or prostitution or become addicted to alcohol or drugs. Many runaways suffer emotional and psychological problems, too.

Various groups offer help to runaway youths. The National Runaway Switchboard runs a telephone crisis hot line. Teens can call for help finding food, shelter, counseling, or health information.

The switchboard also offers the Home Free program, which helps teens who want to go home. And it sets up conference calls for teens who want to contact parents or other agencies.

Other organizations operate shelters. These are places where teens can feel safe and warm and be fed. Because federal funding is limited, the number of runaways far exceeds the number of shelter beds.

In any case, shelters are not a long-term solution for runaways. One fifteen-year-old girl ran away because her alcoholic mother beat her. She felt safer at a shelter in Westchester County, New York.

But federal funding restrictions meant she could not stay more than thirty days. The girl did not know where she would go when the time ran out. "I'll go anyplace but home," she vowed.[13]

For this girl and for other runaways, the legal duty to provide a safe home remains with her parents until a state judge rules otherwise. Yet the future looks bleak. After all, serious problems made her leave in the first place.

Reporting the mother again for abuse is one option. Seeking foster care is another possibility. None of the girl's choices comes anywhere close to living "happily ever after."

Can Teens Divorce Their Parents?

Fifteen years ago people would have laughed at the idea of children divorcing parents. The state could sometimes terminate a parent's rights, but no one thought that a child could do so.

In a few cases, however, courts have let young people sever ties with their natural parents. These cases are rare, yet they signal important changes.

Until he was twelve, Gregory Kingsley bounced around. His natural parents were separated. Sometimes he lived with one of them. Other times, he lived in foster care.

One time Ralph Kingsley, his natural father, was charged with abusing and neglecting Gregory and his brothers. Life with the mother, Rachel Kingsley, was not much better. Witnesses said she often left the boys alone. Other testimony showed that she often drank too much alcohol and smoked marijuana. Testimony showed she sometimes slapped her sons on their heads.[14]

Florida lawyer George Russ first glimpsed Gregory at a Florida children's residence. He and his wife, Lizabeth Russ, already had eight children. "But I couldn't get him off my mind," George Russ said.[15]

First, the couple visited Gregory. Then, they became his foster parents. In October 1991, Gregory came to live with the Russ family.

Gregory asked George and Lizabeth Russ to adopt him. The couple agreed, but Gregory's natural mother objected. She refused to consent. Gregory hired attorney Jerri Blair to represent him, and the case went to court.

The hearing took two days. The judge asked why Gregory wanted to sever legal ties with his biological mother. Gregory answered, "I'm doing it for me, so I can be happy."[16]

Judge Thomas Kirk terminated the biological mother's rights as a parent. That let the adoption go forward. Gregory changed his name to Shawn Russ and proudly donned a new "RUSS #9" shirt. He was now the family's ninth child.[17]

Fifteen-year-old Kimberly Mays also severed ties with her natural parents, the Twiggs. Kimberly was accidentally switched at birth with another girl, Arlena, whose natural parents were the Mayses. Each girl went home to the other girl's parents.[18] Kimberly was raised by Robert Mays after his wife died.

After Arlena died from a heart defect, her medical records showed that she could not have been the Twiggs's natural daughter. The Twiggs investigated and discovered the hospital switch.

At first, the Twiggs and Mays families agreed that Kimberly would visit the Twiggs regularly. But soon Kimberly felt the Twiggs wanted to turn her against the father who had raised her, Robert Mays. She wanted to end all the visits.

Kimberly hired George Russ (Shawn's adoptive father) as her attorney and went to court. She wanted to end all legal connection with her natural parents.

"Are you sure you don't want to see any of them again?" the Twiggs's lawyer asked Kimberly at trial. "I am positively sure," Kimberly testified in court.[19] The court ruled in Kimberly's favor.

Another case involved Sonya Kinney, a fifteen-year-old girl who was deaf. Her divorced parents refused to learn sign language. Instead, they communicated with her by stomping or shouting. Neither method worked well at all.[20]

Being unable to communicate is frustrating in any case. For Sonya, it was terrifying. She claimed that her mother's new husband sexually abused her. But neither parent could "listen" to her charges.[21]

North Carolina judge Shelly Holt granted custody to Sonya's sign-language interpreter, Joanie Hughes. "I'm saved," Sonya said in sign language.[22]

Such cases are quite rare. Most teens do not "divorce" their parents. But the cases are important. They show that courts do not always defer to parents. Teens are gaining a greater say in their family life.

Emancipation

Emancipation declares that emancipated teens are legally free from their parents. They can make their own decisions because legally they are considered adults.[23]

Sometimes emancipation occurs automatically. If a teen under eighteen marries with parental consent, the parents no longer have responsibility for the teen. The teen and spouse are both considered legal adults. They become their own family.

Likewise, if a teen joins the armed forces before reaching age eighteen, a parent's consent is required. After that, the teen is a legal adult.

Teens or parents can also ask a court to order emancipation, as Dominique Moceanu did. Courts look at each case's facts. Where has the teen been living? Who has provided financial support for the teen? Does the minor own property and pay his or her own debts? Is the minor claimed as a dependent on the parent's tax return?

Maturity is also a factor. Once a teen becomes a

legal adult, no one has a legal duty to care for him or her. The teen must be able to make wise choices about where to live, how to obtain medical care, how to manage money, and other factors. Thus, courts weigh the question of maturity carefully.

Emancipation comes with a price. True, parents can no longer dictate the terms of a teen's life, but the parents no longer have any duty to provide financial support, either. The teen can no longer rely on parents for food, shelter, clothing, costs related to school, or other expenses. The responsibilities of earning an income, paying bills, and providing for life's necessities fall squarely on the teen's shoulders. This takes not only maturity but also resources that are beyond the means of many teens.

Wrapping Up

In summary, teens at home usually must obey their parents. Courts in most cases defer to the parents on discipline, chores, privacy matters, and privileges.

Parents must provide basic needs for children: food, clothing, shelter, and medical care. Failure to provide these is considered neglect. Parents also cannot physically or sexually abuse their children.

If abuse or neglect occurs, courts and social agencies can take action. The system is not perfect, but teens who need help can pursue options.

Teens who run away from home face huge problems. Resources such as the National Runaway Switchboard can provide help.

Some teens go to court to ask a judge to hear their

case and declare them emancipated. The process is rather unusual. If granted, emancipation makes the teen a legal adult. The teen must then provide all of his or her own basic needs.

Even more unusual are cases letting teens "divorce" their parents. While rare, the cases show that courts care about teens' personal interests. Special circumstances get special treatment.

3

Teens and
Their Bodies

Parents must provide children with necessary health care. Children need vaccinations for school. They need medical treatment after an accident. They need care when they are ill. Seeing to this is part of a parent's job.

A Parent's Role in Medical Care

Most parents make the major decisions about their children's health. They decide when children should see the doctor. They consult with the doctor. They give consent for medical treatment.

Consent is permission for medical

treatment. Treatment may be the probing of an exam, prescribing medicines, or surgery.

In any case, all licensed health practitioners need informed consent forms, meaning a person understands what is going on. The health professional must explain the illness and the treatment risks.

For example, a medicine may have side effects or surgery might not succeed. The patient must accept those risks as part of the treatment. Otherwise, the patient might sue the health professional later if things go wrong.

When treating minors, health care providers usually ask parents to sign informed consent forms.[1] They want to avoid arguments down the road in case the parents later disagree with the treatment.

Special arrangements ensure that children receive treatment in an emergency even if parents are not around. Suppose a child gets hurt at school. School and emergency personnel can give first aid. A hospital can give emergency treatment to save a life or stabilize the child's condition. Most schools require parents to sign a form each year stating whether they authorize emergency treatment.

Withholding consent on the form can delay treatment while the health care provider locates the parents. But even without parental consent, health care providers must take life-saving measures.

Fortunately, most parents want to provide good health care for their children. However, parents often fail to provide necessary medical treatment. Some are negligent and mistreat the child.

Other parents do not give children medical care

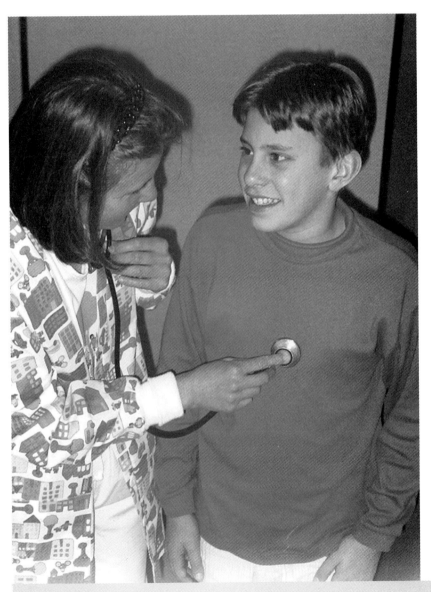

Minors often need parental consent for medical treatment.

because of their religious beliefs. In one case, a Minnesota boy had diabetes, which requires insulin to treat it. Instead of taking the boy to the doctor, the mother and stepfather took him to a faith healer. The faith healer did not give the boy insulin. Instead, the three adults prayed for the boy. Sadly, he died.

Then the boy's natural father sued. In *Lundman* v. *McKown*, a Minnesota court ruled that the mother and stepfather acted unlawfully. It ordered them and the faith healer to pay $1.5 million to the father.[2]

A few states have "religious shield" laws that defer to the parents' religious beliefs. Despite this, the *Lundman* case is now the law in most states. Most courts say parents must get life-saving treatment for minors—regardless of religious beliefs. Parents must save the child's life.[3]

Teens' Own Health Decisions

Maturing teens face new health issues. They want an active role in their own health decisions.

Ideally, teens will talk with parents about health questions. Yet even teens who get along with their parents may feel uncomfortable about some issues. Can teens get medical care on their own?

Most states require parental consent. But exceptions are important. Some states let teens consent to any health care even before they turn eighteen. Other states let teens consent to certain types of care.

"These laws do vary state by state, and they also change a little bit from time to time," notes attorney Abigail English, director of the Center for Adolescent Health and the Law in Chapel Hill, North Carolina.[4]

English encourages teens to check with a local health clinic or doctor. They will know the specifics of a particular state's laws.

Some states have a "mature minor" doctrine. The health care provider must judge if the teen is mature enough to make informed decisions. If so, the teen can give consent.[5] The doctrine applies even if the teen is not emancipated from his or her parents.

The mature minor doctrine applies more to outpatient treatment. Inpatient hospital care is expensive. Most teens do not have their own health insurance. To ensure coverage by the parents' insurance, hospitals usually require parental consent.[6]

Even in states without the mature minor doctrine, doctors owe teens confidentiality. They must keep information about the patient's health private, unless they have the teen's permission to tell others.[7] Many parents understand this and give general consent for the family doctor to treat teen children.[8]

Other parents are surprised. "You'll have to ask them if it's all right for me to discuss that," one nurse told parents who wanted information.[9]

Confidentiality is not absolute; there are exceptions. Some states' laws let doctors judge whether to inform parents. Other conditions, such as possible child abuse, may require notification to authorities. "It's a good idea to ask your health care provider what kind of confidentiality protection there is," says English.[10]

Alcohol and Substance Abuse

Beyond this, most states let teens arrange for their own health care in special circumstances. In these cases, advance parental consent might deter teens from getting care. Rather than have teens forgo care, the law wants to help.[11]

Alcohol and substance abuse are serious problems. Since the 1980s, teens in most states can get confidential diagnosis and treatment for alcohol and substance abuse problems.[12]

Local telephone directory listings for Alcoholics Anonymous and Narcotics Anonymous are starting points for referrals. A doctor or adolescent health clinic can also give information.

Sexually Transmitted Diseases

Sexually transmitted diseases (STDs) are another serious teen health problem. Studies suggest that between 40 and 50 percent of teen girls and 55 percent of teen boys are sexually active.[13] These teens are at risk for HIV, syphilis, gonorrhea, herpes, human papilloma virus, and other STDs.

Almost all states let teens get diagnosis for STDs without parental consent.[14] Local clinics may even provide treatment for free or at minimal cost.

Some STDs can be cured quickly with antibiotics or other medication. Other conditions, such as herpes, can be treated but require steps to make sure the condition is not spread in the future. Some conditions, such as HIV/AIDS, have no known cure.

The law in most states lets teens get tested for HIV/AIDS. How much treatment they can get after that is unclear. Treatment costs can be staggering, so

Various states let teens who admit that they have an alcohol or substance abuse problem seek medical help on their own.

parents' consent may be needed.[15] The law is still developing, so teens should ask their health clinics.

STDs are serious conditions. They require prompt attention and medical treatment. Teens can ask their physicians or contact the CDC National STD Hotline at (800) 227-8922.

Birth Control, Pregnancy, and Abortion

Sexually active teens run the risk of pregnancy. Many need information about pregnancy and birth control.

"Right now in any state a minor can get contraception based on their own consent and on a confidential basis at a Title X funded clinic," says

Abigail English. "Title X is the federal family planning program, and money gets distributed to all the states."[16] Planned Parenthood, teen health clinics, and similar sources can provide more information.

Despite available information, not all sexually active teens use birth control. And birth control sometimes fails. What happens then?

About four hundred thousand girls under age eighteen become pregnant each year in the United States.[17] Most states let pregnant teens arrange medical care for themselves and their babies.[18]

Also, many states say health care providers owe pregnant teens a duty of confidentiality. They cannot tell parents or others about the pregnancy without the teen's consent. Again, teens should ask any questions about confidentiality when they first seek care.

Once a teen has a baby, she has all the legal duties of a parent to that baby. She must support the baby. The baby's father has support duties, too.[19]

Suppose a pregnant teen wants an abortion. The Supreme Court has held that women can lawfully get abortions.[20] But some states do not automatically let teens get abortions.

More than three dozen states have passed laws calling for parental involvement. These laws say parents need to consent before teens can get abortions. But parents may disagree with a teen's choice. Or a teen might be afraid to involve her parents.[21]

If a teen does not get her parent's consent, then laws restricting teen abortions must allow "judicial bypass." Judicial bypass lets a teen ask a judge to allow the abortion. The teen must persuade the judge that she is mature enough to decide on her own. Or she must convince the court that an abortion is in her best interests. Groups in some states offer adult advocates if teens go to court.[22]

The Supreme Court has held that such laws satisfy the federal Constitution.[23] The laws aim to balance the issue of legal access to an abortion with the fact that the teen is still a minor whose best interests the law wants to protect.

Teens in all states can get birth control. Teens who become pregnant can also generally get care for themselves and their babies. Once teens have children, they are legally responsible for them.

Psychological Problems

Depression, mood swings, and anorexia nervosa are just a few psychological problems that can trouble teens. About half the states let teens get psychological counseling on their own.[24] They can either call a teen health clinic or ask the school psychologist for referral to a counselor.

Some states limit the number of counseling sessions that teens can get on their own. The psychologist or psychiatrist can help the teen decide what to do after that.

Sometimes parents try to force treatment on teens despite their objections. They may drag teens to see a psychologist or psychiatrist, or they may try to get teens admitted to a hospital for treatment.

Some parents are right in seeking such care. Yet one Children's Defense Fund study showed that about 40 percent of juvenile admissions to mental health institutions were not proper.[25]

To guard against this, teens have a legal right to review by an appointed professional. A social services caseworker or someone appointed by the court reviews the case. He or she must be neutral—that is, the reviewer does not have a stake in who wins.

If the reviewer sides with the teen, treatment cannot be forced. If the reviewer agrees with the parents, the teen can be admitted involuntarily for counseling. In *Parham* v. *J. R.*, the United States Supreme Court ruled that this was constitutional.[26]

Thus, most states let teens get at least some psychological help on their own. But parents might also decide that teens need psychological help. If the teen objects, parents cannot force treatment unless a neutral psychological professional reviews the case.

Can Teens Refuse Medical Treatment?

In Coral Springs, Florida, fifteen-year-old Benny was sick. He had already received two liver transplants. His body started rejecting the second liver. Doctors increased Benny's medications. The medications were supposed to keep his body from rejecting the liver, but the side effects made Benny feel worse.

Benny stopped taking the medications. He knew it meant he would die, but he was tired of the awful side effects. Benny said his doctors did not realize how bad his pain was. "[T]hey would never realize it, unless they were going through it themselves," he said, "but their job is to keep their patients alive for as long as they can."[27]

Benny's parents sided with his decision. The Florida Department of Health and Rehabilitative Services disagreed. It put Benny in the hospital and tried to force him to take the medications. Benny and his parents asked the court for help.

Florida judge Arthur Birken listened to Benny's doctors. He also talked with Benny at the hospital. Finally, Judge Birken ruled that Benny could refuse the medications. The hospital released him. Two months later, Benny died.[28]

The American Academy of Pediatrics says that physicians should respect young patients' rights to refuse certain treatments.[29] But Benny's case was unusual. Most courts do not let teens refuse life-saving treatments.

Sixteen-year-old Gregory Novak fell asleep while driving. His car crashed into a guardrail on an inter-state highway in Georgia. He was rushed to the hospital. He needed a blood transfusion.

Both Gregory and his mother objected. For reli-gious reasons, they did not want a blood transfusion. So the court named another adult as a guardian. The court let that adult consent to the transfusion, despite Gregory's and his mother's objections. In *Novak* v. *Cobb County Kennestone Hospital Authority*, a federal court upheld the action.[30]

Experts disagree on whether teens are mature enough to make life or death decisions.[31] Judges usu-ally want to err on the side of caution. Most courts will probably require life-saving treatments.

What Say Do Schools Have?

Teens have some say about their health and their bodies. So do parents. But what about schools? What say do they have about teens' health decisions?

If students pose a health risk to others, schools can exclude them from regular classes. A student with a highly contagious disease, for example, can be sent home. If the illness continues, many districts offer an alternative, such as home tutoring.

Just being sick does not automatically mean that a student is a health risk. In 1986 an Indiana school district tried to keep teen Ryan White out of school because he had AIDS. But AIDS cannot be caught by just sitting in the same classroom with someone. So Ryan went to court. He won the right to attend regular high school classes.[32]

Schools can also keep students out of regular classes if their behavior is a threat. Generally, the school must have an alternate plan, such as special education classes. And the school must get the parents' consent. Otherwise, the parents can ask for independent review of the school's plan for the teen.

Sometimes schools may suspect that a student's health is in danger at home. Frequent bruises or broken bones might be signs of physical abuse. Other conditions may suggest sexual abuse.

If the student could be in physical danger, schools must act. State laws require schools to notify social services when they have reason to believe a minor may be abused.[33]

The duty to report applies even if the teen does

not want others to know. Also, parents cannot sue school personnel for reporting suspected abuse as long as the report was made in good faith.[34]

Substance abuse is a serious health problem. Schools can ban alcohol and drugs from school property. They can bar students from coming to school under the influence of these substances. Schools can search for drugs and alcohol. And schools can notify parents and require treatment when they suspect that a teen has a substance abuse problem.

Schools can forbid students from engaging in sexual activity at school. But federal law says public schools cannot punish girls who get pregnant. Teen mothers who want to continue school can do so.[35]

Public schools cannot punish teen mothers, but can they withhold privileges? At Grant County High School in Kentucky, Somer Chipman and Chastity Glass were the only juniors with high grades who were kept out of the school's National Honor Society chapter. Both were unwed teen mothers.[36]

"Character" is a criterion for admission to the prestigious honor society. But the National Honor Society's official handbook said pregnancy is not a basis for automatic denial.[37] In December 1998, a federal judge ordered the school to admit the girls to the National Honor Society.[38]

Wrapping Up

Parents have a duty to provide medical care for teens. In most cases, parents must consent to medical care for their children. But important exceptions apply. These exceptions vary from state to state.

Some states let mature minors consent to their own medical treatment. In other cases, the duty of confidentiality may protect teens from having their health information told to others.

Even in states that do not have the mature minor doctrine, teens can consent to health care in special cases. Almost all states let teens get some care for alcohol and substance abuse, sexually transmitted diseases, birth control, and pregnancy. Some states place conditions on teen abortions. Teens may also get psychological counseling on their own in some states. On the other hand, parents cannot commit teens to an institution without independent review.

A few court cases have been decided in favor of teens who refused medical treatment. In most cases, however, courts are likely to require life-saving measures for minors.

Schools have some say in teens' health. They can keep students who present a significant risk out of regular classes. They can keep drugs and alcohol off school property. They can regulate conduct on school property. And they *must* tell authorities if they think a student is in danger of abuse at home.

But public schools' say is limited. In particular, they cannot discriminate against teens who become pregnant. And they cannot readily control behavior that occurs entirely off school grounds. Schools can teach students about good health practices, but they cannot control everything students choose to do.

4

The Rules
at School

The most basic right at school is the right
to learn. Nothing guarantees honor roll or
good grades. Teens also have the right to
an education at public expense.

This chapter focuses on rights at public schools. Public schools are run by local
and state governments. School administrators and teachers must obey the United
States Constitution.

Teens at private schools can be treated
differently. Their parents choose to send
them there. Within limits, their parents
can agree to stricter rules. However, even
private schools must observe some basic
student rights. Many private schools get

41

some federal funds—such as for school lunches. So these schools must comply with the federal law on access to student records, for example. Funding eligibility can also require schools not to discriminate on the basis of race.

Private schools can also be subject to state licensing laws. These laws determine what minimum requirements a school must meet to qualify as an approved school under state education laws. State law would say how many years of any subject a high school student must have to get a diploma.

In other ways, however, teens at private schools can be treated differently from public school students. Their parents' choice to send them there amounts to agreement with whatever stricter rules the private school makes. Thus, for example, disciplinary rules and dress codes at private schools can be stricter than their counterparts in public schools.

Harassment From Other Students

Can any teen get a good education in a school plagued by harassment and discrimination? Federal laws forbids school employees from discriminating against students on the basis of race, religion, and gender. If they do discriminate, they can be sued.

Sadly, the worst harassment can come from other students. Name-calling and teasing can escalate into pinching, grabbing, groping, and other attacks.[1]

In Forsyth, Georgia, a student named G. F. repeatedly touched fifth-grader LaShonda. The student said he wanted to have sex with her. Each time,

LaShonda and her mother told school officials. Officials never disciplined G. F. Finally, LaShonda's mother, Aurelia Davis, complained to the county sheriff. G. F. was arrested. He pleaded guilty to sexual battery.[2]

Meanwhile, LaShonda's grades had dipped. Her mental health suffered. Still angered by the school's inaction, LaShonda's mother sued. She claimed the school committed sexual discrimination against LaShonda by failing to stop the harassment.

In May 1999 the Supreme Court allowed the suit to go forward.[3] This meant that the trial court could not dismiss the case. Instead, it had to hear the evidence and decide the case on its merits.

LaShonda won a real victory in *Davis* v. *Monroe County Board of Education*. Her case means that schools cannot ignore complaints about sexual harassment.

The Court's reasoning also applies to racial or other types of harassment. Proving harassment is difficult. But courts can force schools to pay damages if the schools know about and ignore harassment.

Teens have a right to an education. That right includes freedom from harassment and discrimination.

Fair Treatment and Student Files

Teens and their parents have a right to see the permanent record maintained by the school. Until teens are eighteen, the right technically belongs to parents, but most high schools let teens see their own records.[4]

Each teen's record has a transcript of classes and grades. Also included is information about disciplinary actions, college admissions, and scholarships. Counselors' reports, some health data, and family history may also appear. Records might also include personal comments from various teachers and staff.

Before releasing information, schools usually need permission from teens or their parents, or a court order. When teens apply to college, the school grants permission to release the records. Employers, banks, credit card companies, and even the police may also ask to see school records.

Teens who have any concerns can arrange to review their records in advance. If they find an error, they can ask for a correction or supply a written explanation for the file.[5]

School Discipline

Children and teens must attend school until a certain age, or be in an approved alternative, such as home-schooling.

Compulsory education laws apply until teens reach age fifteen through eighteen; the exact age depends on the state.[6] Exceptions apply for families with certain religious beliefs.[7]

While attending school, teens must do classwork and homework. If they do not, teachers can lower their grades. They can even fail a student.

About 10 percent of high schools require teens to do community service.[8] Activities vary from collecting items for homeless people, to tutoring, to helping clean up litter.

"There is no better way to teach and reinforce honesty, respect, tolerance, work ethic, discipline, self-respect, and respect for others,"[9] explained Chicago school chief Paul Vallas. Many students enjoy the community service experience. They like helping others and learn valuable skills.

But some people disagree. "I have no problem with community service," said student John Reinhard, Jr. "But if you force someone to do it, don't call it volunteering."[10] John and his father sued the Chapel Hill School District in North Carolina. The state court upheld the school's requirement.[11]

Teens must obey school rules even if they do not always agree with them. Schools can enforce their rules strictly as long as they act evenhandedly.

In Fairborn, Ohio, Baker Junior High School has a "zero-tolerance" policy when it comes to drugs. One eighth-grade honor student gave her friend Midol™ at school. Midol is legally sold as an over-the-counter medicine. However, Baker Junior High School's rules do not allow students to carry or give other students any medications at all, unless supervised or approved by the school nurse. Because the girls violated the rules, the school suspended them. The students appealed, but a federal court upheld the school's enforcement of its zero-tolerance policy.[12]

What happens when teachers say students violated school rules? In Columbus, Ohio, a lunchroom disturbance erupted at Central High School. At least seventy-five students were suspended. One student,

Dwight Lopez, said he was just a bystander. No one let him tell his side of the story first.

At nearby Marion Franklin High School, a student demonstration disrupted a school program. Tyrone Washington and Rudolph Sutton were suspended for ten days, with no chance to explain.

Together with six other students, Dwight, Tyrone, and Rudolph sued the Columbus schools. In *Goss* v. *Lopez*, the Supreme Court ruled that the schools deprived the teens of their constitutional rights.[13]

Specifically, the students had a right to an education. The schools could not take that right away without due process—rules designed to ensure fair treatment. The Court wrote,

> Neither the property interest in educational benefits temporarily denied nor the liberty interest in reputation, which is also implicated, is so insubstantial that suspensions may constitutionally be imposed by any procedure the school chooses, no matter how arbitrary.[14]

At a minimum, students subject to suspension must be told the charges against them. Then they have a chance to tell their side of the story. If practical, the hearing should be held before any suspension. Otherwise, it should be held as soon as possible afterward.[15]

When is a prior hearing impractical? T. P. got into a fight at Greene-Taliaferro Comprehensive High School in Georgia. She screamed obscenities. When told to stop, she refused to calm down. A teacher carried T. P. to the principal's office. There, T. P. threatened to kill the other girl in the fight. She also assaulted the principal. T. P. was suspended for nine days.

T. P. and her mother later told the principal in a phone call that another student had started the fight. However, the principal refused to lift the suspension. The court decided that the school had provided T. P. with sufficient due process, and the suspension was justified.[16] A longer suspension would have required a more formal hearing.

Expulsion is more serious than suspension. It removes a student permanently from the school. Public schools must provide students with a formal hearing before taking this drastic remedy.

At the other end of the disciplinary spectrum are after-school detentions or punishment assignments. One example would be an essay on "Why Talking in Class Is Wrong." These actions can wind up in a teen's permanent record. Schools generally do not have to provide a formal or informal hearing before such punishments.

Corporal Punishment

Can schools use corporal punishment, such as spanking or striking? The answer depends on where a student lives. Some states say no; others say yes—within limits.

James Ingraham attended junior high school in Dade County, Florida. At one point, James was paddled so hard that he missed eleven days of school. James and another student sued. They argued that physical punishment was cruel and unusual punishment, which is forbidden by the Eighth Amendment to the United States Constitution.

The Supreme Court disagreed. In *Ingraham* v. *Wright*, the Court held that corporal punishment is not a violation of the Eighth Amendment. "Teachers may impose reasonable but not excessive force to discipline a child," wrote the Supreme Court.[17]

Corporal punishment can still violate other constitutional rights, such as due process rights under the Fifth and Fourteenth Amendments.[18] The more severe the punishment, the more likely it will be held unlawful.

N. B. and some friends were talking in the school parking lot after a football game. N. B. disliked one quarterback who always insisted on getting his own way. To illustrate his point, N. B. said, "Heil Hitler." He was mocking the quarterback. Just then, the principal walked by. He thought N. B. was talking about him. Immediately the principal grabbed N. B. He squeezed his neck, causing purple bruises. N. B. needed treatment at the emergency room.

The police arrested the principal and charged him with assault. Then N. B.'s father, P. B., sued the principal for damages on his son's behalf. Damages are money paid to compensate someone for an injury. In *P.B.* v. *Koch*, a federal court held the principal's force was unreasonable. Thus, he could be liable for damages.[19]

What force is reasonable? Two sixteen-year-old girls were screaming and cursing at each other at Batavia High School in Kane County, Illinois. A business teacher told both girls to sit, but they kept arguing. When the teacher told one girl, Heather, to leave, she lingered.

The teacher grabbed Heather's wrist to lead her away. She told him to let go, and he did. Heather left the classroom, slamming the door.

Heather then sued the teacher. A federal court ruled that the teacher's actions were not corporal punishment. Rather, they were meant to keep order in the classroom. Even if grabbing the wrist were punishment, the Court ruled, the teacher's actions were reasonable. "This most emphatically is not a matter rising to the level of a constitutional violation."[20]

Aside from constitutional issues, state law can restrict punishments. As of 1995, the twenty states that had passed laws banning corporal punishment were: Alaska, California, Connecticut, Hawaii, Iowa, Maine, Massachusetts, Michigan, Nebraska, New Hampshire, New Jersey, New York, North Dakota, Oregon, Rhode Island, South Dakota, Vermont, Virginia, Wisconsin, and the District of Columbia.[21]

These laws mean that even if a spanking or slap does not cause serious harm, the teacher may not do it. Some local school districts also forbid corporal punishment. Students can check with local school boards to learn what specific laws apply to them.

Student Searches

The Fourth Amendment protects against unreasonable searches by the government. Before a search, the police need probable cause to believe a crime was committed. Often the police also need a search warrant. At school, however, a lower standard applies.

In New Jersey, a teacher accused fourteen-year-old T. L. O. of smoking cigarettes in the lavatory. The girl vigorously denied it. Assistant Principal Thomas Choplick listened to the teacher's suspicions. Then he opened T. L. O.'s purse. Inside, he found cigarettes. Choplick also found marijuana and rolling papers. There was also a list of names. Apparently, T. L. O. had sold marijuana to the people named on her list. The police brought delinquency charges against T. L. O. She claimed that the public school violated her constitutional rights.

In *New Jersey* v. *T.L.O.*, the Supreme Court ruled in favor of the school district.[22] The Court said public school students have some privacy rights, but making teachers get warrants before searches "would unduly interfere with the maintenance of the swift and informal disciplinary procedures needed in the schools."[23] The assistant principal's search was lawful under the Fourth Amendment.

A cigarette search also caused a stir at Orange Glen High School in Escondido, California. The vice principal knew some students in a group had smoked. He did not know which ones, though. To find out, he herded them all into school. Then each student was searched.

Sixteen-year-old Beth Ann Smith did not have cigarettes. She had three knives. One double-edged dagger had a four-inch blade. The police filed charges against Beth Ann. At trial, the juvenile court judge

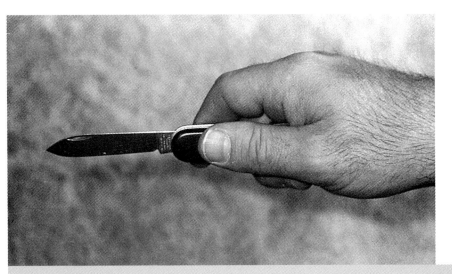

Carrying knives or other weapons can lead to suspension or expulsion, according to school rules.

kept the knives out of evidence. Beth Ann was released.

Then Beth Ann sued. The federal court said she had no claim. Generally, public-school officials are immune from claims if they act in good faith. In fact, the search had been lawful. So the school had acted in good faith. Beth Ann lost her case.[24]

Can schools use metal detectors for searches? At Granby High School in Norfolk, Virginia, the school's magnometer sounded over 90 percent of the time. In effect, students argued, school officials used it for random searches of students. The American Civil Liberties Union of Virginia filed suit. The state court sided with the school.[25]

When are searches too intrusive? At Liberty High

School in Issaquah, Washington, a student claimed he was missing one hundred dollars. School officials searched fifteen boys. They made ten of them take off their clothes, strip-searching them. No one had the money.

After several students sued, the school changed its search policy. It also paid the students $34,000 in damages.[26]

Locker searches are far less intrusive. Harbor Creek High School in Erie, Pennsylvania, conducted random locker searches. Evidence led to a student's arrest on marijuana charges. The Pennsylvania Supreme Court ruled that the locker searches were lawful.[27]

In short, schools may conduct searches to see that rules are followed. Schools have more authority to search students than police have to search citizens. Yet some searches, such as strip searches, can go too far.

Drug Testing

Schools cannot force every student to take a drug test. However, schools can make drug tests a condition of many student privileges.

School board members in Vernonia, Oregon, worried about athletes' drug use. Drugs could cause potentially dangerous errors at school sporting events. Besides, other students respected the school athletes. School board members wanted them to set a good example.

The school board decided to require random drug

Can school personnel search the personal stuff in a student's locker? Under various circumstances, the answer is yes.

testing of all student athletes. To participate in sports, students had to consent to the testing.

Students had to provide urine samples while an adult remained in the room. Samples went to a lab. There, they were tested for amphetamines, cocaine, marijuana, and alcohol.

Seventh-grader James Acton wanted to play football, but he balked at the drug testing. Why? "Because I feel that they have no reason to think I was taking drugs," James said.[28]

James was a good student with no history of discipline problems. Instead of taking the test, James and his parents filed suit. They argued that the rule violated James's Fourth Amendment right to be free from unreasonable searches and seizures.

The Supreme Court upheld the drug testing program in *Vernonia School District 47J* v. *Acton*.[29] "The effects of a drug-infested school are visited not just upon the users," wrote Justice Antonin Scalia in 1995, "but upon the entire student body and faculty, as the educational process is disrupted."[30]

The Court stressed that Vernonia's program was limited. It applied only to school athletes, "where the risk of immediate physical harm to the drug user or those with whom he is playing his sport is particularly high."[31]

Matthew Todd did not want to play football. He just wanted to videotape the games at Rushville Consolidated High School in Indiana. In August 1996, the school board adopted a new policy. It required students in any school activities to agree to random urine tests for drugs. Students also had to consent if they wanted to drive to and from school.

The school did not need suspicion of wrongdoing before requiring a drug test. If results were positive, a student could explain them. For example, the student might be taking certain prescription medicines. Otherwise, the student was barred from club activities or driving. Only by passing another test could the student regain these privileges.

Matthew refused to take the test, so he was banned from videotaping the football team. Other students who would not take the drug tests were kept out of the Library Club and Future Farmers of America. In January 1998 a federal court ruled that the testing program did not violate the students' rights.[32]

While the Rushville and Vernonia testing programs affected many students, they were not universal. A Dade County, Florida, policy approved random testing for all students, beginning in 1998. But students still could not be tested unless parents consented. Also, positive tests would not result in school or criminal penalties.[33]

Not all drug testing challenges fail. High school freshman James Willis was suspended in December 1997. He had fought with another student. When James refused to provide urine for a drug test, Anderson High School suspended him again. They also threatened to expel him.

In 1998 the Seventh Circuit Court of Appeals ruled in James's favor. "In *Vernonia* and *Todd*, drug testing could be construed as part of the 'bargain' a student strikes in exchange for the privilege of participating in favored activities," the court reasoned.[34] In contrast, there was nothing voluntary in the threat of expulsion.[35]

Wrapping Up

Every state requires teens to attend school until a particular age, which varies from state to state. Students attending public school are entitled to a free education at public expense.

Schools must act fairly. They cannot discriminate on the basis of race, religion, or gender. As a way to ensure fairness, federal law allows review of students' permanent files. Parents and students can request corrections or add to the record if they feel it is wrong.

Schools can adopt rules for students, and students must comply with reasonable rules. Rules help create an atmosphere for learning.

When students break valid rules, schools can take action. Significant disciplinary actions, such as suspensions and expulsions, require hearings. The type of hearing depends on the severity of the punishment.

Some states allow corporal punishment. Other states ban it. Even in states that allow corporal punishment, unreasonable physical force may be cause for a lawsuit against school personnel.

Schools can conduct searches to make sure rules are followed. Search warrants are not required, but schools do have to act reasonably.

Recent federal cases allow schools to require drug

tests in some cases. There must be some "voluntary" element. Sports and club activities are considered "voluntary" in this sense—even though they are a central part of many students' school experiences. Individual states may impose additional restrictions on drug testing or other searches.

5

Freedom of Expression

The First Amendment to the United States Constitution guarantees freedom of speech and of the press. It also guarantees freedom of religion and the right to associate with other people. What happens when teen opinions clash with school administrators' views?

Protesting a War

In 1965 the Vietnam War embroiled America in controversy. John and Mary Beth Tinker and their friend Christopher Eckhardt wore black armbands to protest the war. Thirteen-year-old Mary Beth was

58

sent home from junior high school. Fifteen-year-old John and sixteen-year-old Christopher were suspended from high school until they returned without their armbands. The teens' families sued in federal court.[1]

The school wanted to keep order in the classroom. The school felt the armbands would be disruptive. The students believed that the Constitution protected their right to speak out against the war.

In *Tinker* v. *Des Moines Independent Community School District*, the Supreme Court ruled for the teens. Students are subject to school rules, but, wrote Supreme Court Justice Abe Fortas, they do not "shed their constitutional rights to freedom of speech or expression at the schoolhouse gate."[2] The school could not punish the teens "for a silent, passive expression of opinion, unaccompanied by any disorder or disturbance."[3]

The Court stressed that students' freedom of expression is not absolute. Schools have a right to maintain order. Where does the line get drawn?

Too Hot to Handle

At Bethel High School in Pierce City, Washington, Matthew Fraser nominated his friend Jeff Kuhlman for student government. His speech had no swear words, but it did have several sexual innuendoes. Matthew said:

> I know a man who is firm—he's firm in his pants, he's firm in his shirt, his character is firm—but most . . . of all, his belief in you, the students of Bethel, is firm.

> Jeff Kuhlman is a man who takes his point and pounds it in. . . . He doesn't attack things in spurts—he drives hard, pushing and pushing until finally—he succeeds.
>
> Jeff is a man who will go to the very end—even the climax, for each and every one of you.[4]

Six hundred students listened to the speech. Some laughed and hooted. Others, including some fourteen-year-olds, appeared to be embarrassed.[5] The school suspended Matthew for two days.

In *Bethel School District 403* v. *Fraser*, the Supreme Court sided with the school district. "The constitutional rights of students in public schools are not automatically coextensive with the rights of adults in other settings," the Court stated.[6] Matthew had a right under the First Amendment to state his ideas. But the school had a "countervailing interest in teaching students the boundaries of socially appropriate behavior."[7]

At Hazelwood East High School in St. Louis, Missouri, teens worked hard on the May 13, 1983, issue of the school newspaper. One article was about unwed teen mothers. Another article discussed divorce in students' families.

Just before the newspaper went to press, the school principal cut both stories. He felt the issues were too sensitive. Teens Cathy Kuhlmeier, Lee Ann Tippet, and Leslie Smart sued.

The school won in *Hazelwood School District* v. *Kuhlmeier*.[8] The Supreme Court said the school had a "valid educational purpose." It could limit what students said in its newspaper. "A school must be able to set high standards for the student speech that is disseminated under its auspices," declared the Court.[9] Schools could keep out bad grammar or poorly written pieces. Also, the school could exclude stories that were "unsuitable for immature audiences."[10]

Since *Hazelwood*, schools have censored many stories. These include articles about crime among students, racism, and substance abuse. Even articles about school board elections have been censored.[11]

The Student Press Law Center has worked to pass state laws that guarantee students freedom of the press.[12] Teens can check with the Student Press Law Center to find out if their state has such a law.[13] Otherwise, *Hazelwood* controls. It lets school administrators decide what student journalists publish.

To avoid *Hazelwood*, some student writers turn to "underground newspapers" that are not school-sponsored, or write their own brochures.

Generally, schools cannot limit the content of such "nonschool" materials.[14] However, schools can regulate where and when students distribute them on school grounds.[15]

What about term papers? Ninth-grader Brittney Settle wanted to write about "The Life of Jesus Christ." Her teacher at Dickson County Junior High School in Tennessee had said students could pick any topic that was "interesting, researchable, and decent." Yet she rejected Brittney's subject. Brittney got a zero.[16]

The teacher said she wanted students to do research. But she felt that Brittney already knew a lot

Teachers have broad discretion in evaluating what students write for class.

about the subject. She doubted that Brittney would write objectively. She also felt that any corrections would be seen as criticism of Brittney's beliefs. The school board sided with the teacher.[17]

A federal appeals court said the school did not violate Brittney's rights. According to the court in *Settle* v. *Dickson County School Board*,

> Students do not lose entirely their right to express themselves as individuals in the classroom, but federal courts should exercise particular restraint in classroom conflicts between student and teacher over matters falling within the ordinary authority of the teacher over curriculum and course content.[18]

Access to Information

In the late 1970s, school board members banned certain books from the library of New York's Island Trees High School. The books included *Slaughterhouse-Five, Soul on Ice, Go Ask Alice,* and *A Hero Ain't Nothing But a Sandwich.* One book, *Laughing Boy,* had won a Pulitzer Prize. Yet the school board claimed that the books were "anti-American, anti-Christian, anti-Semitic, and just plain filthy."[19]

Steven Pico and four other students disagreed. They filed suit. In *Board of Education* v. *Pico,* the Supreme Court held that the students could pursue their claim.[20] As Justice William Brennan wrote,

> The right to receive ideas is a necessary predicate to the *recipient's* meaningful exercise of his own rights of speech, press, and political freedom.

Such access prepares students for active and effective participation in the pluralistic, often contentious society in which they will soon be adult members.[21]

At the same time, the Court said that local school districts have broad discretion. According to Justice Harry Blackmun,

School officials must be able to choose one book over another, without outside interference, when the first book is deemed more relevant to the curriculum, or better written, or when one of a host of other politically neutral reasons is present.[22]

Even after *Pico*, controversy continues. In Tempe, Arizona, a parent objected to *The Adventures of*

When the board of education tried to remove these books from the Island Trees High School library, the Supreme Court ruled that the action violated students' First Amendment rights.

Huckleberry Finn because it uses a word that is now considered racially offensive. In 1998 a federal court ruled that the parent could not keep Twain's literary work out of the classroom.[23]

Parents and students generally cannot keep certain books out of schools. Schools enjoy broad discretion in choosing classroom materials. Students have a right to read different viewpoints.

Dress Codes

What are appropriate school clothes? The answer may be jeans and a T-shirt, slacks or a skirt, or maybe even a uniform. Many students see clothing as a way to express their personalities. School administrators often see the issue differently.

School officials may impose reasonable restrictions. Many schools forbid skimpy tube tops, for example. The rules against revealing clothing help maintain an atmosphere for learning.

Schools often spell out dress codes in student handbooks. But rules are not always clear. A Lexington, Kentucky, high school suspended Tiffany Dargavell in 1997. She wore a Hank Williams, Jr., T-shirt with a Confederate flag. The school dress code said nothing specific about the Confederate flag, but administrators argued that the symbol could have a "racist implication."[24]

In South Hadley, Massachusetts, the restrictive dress code banned "obscene, lewd, or vulgar" statements. It also barred messages that demeaned people because of race, sex, color, national origin, or sexual orientation. It also forbade clothing that advertised drugs, alcohol, or tobacco.

Students Jeff and Jon Pyle protested the school's rule by wearing different shirts. "See Dick Drink, See Dick Drive, See Dick Die, Don't Be a Dick," got Jon sent home to change his shirt. But he was allowed to wear a T-shirt reading, "Coed Naked Gerbils—Some People Will Censor Anything."[25]

With help from the American Civil Liberties Union (ACLU), Jon and Jeff sued. The Massachusetts Supreme Court ruled that the dress code violated student rights under state law. The federal constitutional issue was not addressed.[26]

What about ethnic clothing? In Colorado, Aisha Price and Enockina Ocansey wanted to wear Ghanian Kente cloths at graduation. Federal judge Richard Matsch ruled that Arvada High School may constitutionally require traditional caps, gowns, and tassels.[27] Likewise, in Albuquerque, New Mexico, a school system kept seniors from wearing traditional native attire at graduation.[28]

A Matter of Safety?

No one wants to get shot because of an eighty-six-dollar pair of basketball shoes. Nor does anyone want to be caught in the crossfire during the robbery of a designer jacket. These are just two instances in which teens suffered because of what they wore.[29]

To cut down on crime, many schools limit what students can wear. They ban brand-name jackets and expensive shoes and jewelry, gang colors, symbols, and styles. In Michigan a federal court ruled that South Redford School District's ban on gang-related clothing was constitutional.[30]

In Texas, however, a federal court ruled that the New Caney School District violated the First Amendment. The school forbade teens David Chalifoux and Keith Robertson from wearing rosary beads to class. Some gangs may indeed wear rosary beads, but they are also a religious symbol.[31]

Uniforms may be the greatest restriction on how students dress. Once uniforms were found only in private and parochial schools. But in the last decade, some public school districts have started using uniforms. In 1996 President Clinton announced,

> If it means that the schoolrooms will be more orderly, more disciplined, and that our young people will learn to evaluate themselves by what they are on the inside instead of what they're wearing on the outside, then our public schools should be able to require their students to wear school uniforms.[32]

In 1995, one year after Long Beach, California, adopted a mandatory uniform policy, fights and weapons incidents dropped 50 percent.[33] Some public schools in San Antonio, Chicago, Dayton, Oakland, Birmingham, and New York also have adopted uniforms for some or all grade levels.[34]

Other school systems have voluntary uniform policies, which encourage students to wear uniforms. Some cities also pay for uniforms for poor children. Advocates say uniforms eliminate social bias, reduce peer pressure, and build a sense of community.

School uniforms have traditionally been associated with private schools. Now, some public schools also require their students to wear uniforms.

"From the surveys that I've looked at, I am inclined to believe that wearing uniforms makes quite a bit of difference in how people behave," said Reginald Wilson of the American Council on Education.[35]

Not everyone favors uniforms, though. In 1998 the ACLU filed a lawsuit to challenge the school uniform policy in Lancaster County, South Carolina. The federal court refused to keep the policy from going into effect until trial, so ACLU of South Carolina voluntarily dismissed the case. Other cases are pending as this book goes to press.[36]

Wrapping Up

The First Amendment gives teens a right to express their opinions. But schools may control what appears in official school publications. Schools can also limit where and when students may pass out materials.

Schoolteachers and administrators have a lot of say about what is taught in class. On the one hand, teachers may restrict what subjects teens choose for term papers or other projects. On the other hand, courts generally will not let parents or other groups keep certain books or materials out of the schools.

Student clothing can be a form of expression. The Supreme Court has ruled that some dress styles are protected "speech" under the First Amendment.

Court rulings on teen clothing restrictions vary. Many courts defer to schools. Others say restrictions go too far.

Uniforms in public schools are a fairly new development. Courts have yet to rule definitively on them.

6

Going Online

A few keystrokes, clicks, and a modem are all a person needs to connect to the Internet via computer. This computer network links libraries and databases around the world.

On the Internet, teens can do research or get news and sports scores. They can listen to music, view pictures, and even download computer programs.

The Internet is a communication tool, too. People can send e-mail across town or around the world in just seconds. They can "chat" with online friends and acquaintances. They can post messages on electronic bulletin boards.

70

The Information Superhighway

Welcome to the Information Superhighway. The Internet has revolutionized how people get information and communicate with each other.

The Internet began in 1969 as ARAPNET. It first linked military, defense contractors, and universities doing defense research. Even if a war destroyed normal communications channels, these groups could still communicate.[1]

ARAPNET's military purpose faded away, but the format survived. Now private and government computers around the world communicate with each other. As of 1996, 9.4 million "host" computers were on the Internet. They stored data and relayed communications.[2]

A 1998 study predicts that by 2002, 11 million teens will be online. Another 20 million children under age thirteen will be online, too.[3] The Internet presents incredible technological opportunities. It also poses new questions about teen rights.

Indecent and Obnoxious?

The Internet has a wealth of educational and cultural material. It also has lots of junk and material that may be offensive. Many sites contain sexual images; others use crass language. These sites offend many parents, educators, and religious groups.

Many sexually explicit Web pages contain warnings about their content. But both teens and adults can come across links to these pages accidentally.

Searches for some innocent terms turned up hard-core pornography sites with titillating titles.[4]

Mature teens use judgment. They refrain from viewing offensive Web pages. But parents and others often worry. They do not want their children exposed to obscene Internet sites.

These worries have received government attention. Congress passed the Communications Decency Act in 1996. The law made it a crime to knowingly send "obscene," "patently offensive," or "indecent" materials over the Internet to anyone under age eighteen.

Almost immediately, dozens of groups filed court challenges. Among them were the American Civil Liberties Union, the Electronic Frontier Foundation, Planned Parenthood Federation of America, Inc., Apple Computer, Inc., America Online, Inc., Microsoft Corporation, and the American Library Association.[5]

In *Reno* v. *American Civil Liberties Union* (*Reno I*, 1997), the Supreme Court ruled that the law's "patently offensive" and "indecent" provisions violated the First Amendment.[6] Writing for the majority, Justice John Paul Stevens declared,

> It is true that we have repeatedly recognized the governmental interest in protecting children from harmful materials. But that interest does not justify an unnecessarily broad suppression of speech addressed to adults. . . . In protecting children, the level of discourse reaching a mailbox simply cannot be limited to that which would be suitable for a sandbox.[7]

Despite *Reno I*, some Internet transmissions remain illegal. Material that would be considered obscene or pornographic in print media is still unlawful if someone in the United States sends it over the Internet. Child pornography is a prime example. Another example is obscene e-mail that is sent to annoy someone.[8]

In 1998 Congress passed a narrower, but similar, law.[9] Court challenges followed. In November 1998 the federal district court granted a temporary order in the *Reno II* case. It prevented enforcement of the new law until the case was finally resolved. As this book goes to press, the case is still pending.[10]

Filters

Despite the ruling in *Reno I*, the Supreme Court admitted that parents have an interest in protecting children from objectionable material. What restrictions are allowed?

The Supreme Court said parents could protect children from objectionable Web sites with filtering programs. Companies sell these programs with names like SurfWatch™, NetNanny™, and Cyber Patrol™. Filters block computer access to thousands of sites that meet criteria specified by the program.

Parents can certainly buy these programs. Teen use of the home computer is a privilege. Parents can lawfully condition that privilege on using a filter.

May public libraries or schools use filtering software? After the Communications Decency Act was ruled unconstitutional, congressional lawmakers introduced filter bills. The legislative proposals would require the software for all public libraries and schools receiving federal funds for Internet access.[11]

The American Civil Liberties Union (ACLU) objected.[12] So did Peacefire, a teen Internet advocacy group started by Vanderbilt University student Bennett Haselton.[13] They claimed that filtering software removes discretion from parents to guide children in safe Internet use. The groups also said the software censors far too broadly.

For example, one program blocked the Web site of the American Family Association, a conservative religious group. Why? The group's Web page used the word *homosexuality* in text that criticized certain sexual practices.[14]

Meanwhile, in Alexandria, Virginia, the Loudoun County Public Library Board installed X-Stop™ filtering software. Librarians already chose which books and magazines to purchase, so the library board felt it could choose to access only Internet materials that satisfied the software. "We gave them [the public] what they wanted," said board member Mary Ellen VanNederynen, "a safe place for their kids."[15]

Various Web-site promoters sued. They included the American Association of University Women (Maryland chapter) and Jeremy Myers's Books for Gay and Lesbian Teens Youth Page.

In 1998, district court judge Leonie Brinkema, a former librarian, struck down the policy. "The Library Board may not adopt and enforce content-based restrictions on access to protected Internet speech," wrote Judge Brinkema, unless the named restrictions meet the highest level of constitutional scrutiny.[16]

The ACLU and American Library Association applauded the decision. The National Law Center for Children and Families claimed it made "our public libraries the only adult bookstores open to our grandchildren."[17]

The judge did not say that libraries could never use filters. For example, filter software might only affect terminals used by children. That would still let adults have access to everything on the Internet.

Loudoun County Public Library changed its policy. It removed the filters. Then it set up screens around Internet terminals telling minors that they must get their parents' permission to use the Internet.

In another case, a Livermore, California, parent tried to force a public library to use filters. Otherwise, she said, the facility was a public nuisance. In January 1999 the Alameda County Superior Court dismissed the lawsuit. It ruled that the parent had no claim.[18]

Until there is a clear national standard, schools and libraries can adopt different policies. As of 1998, the Cleveland Public Library in Ohio did not restrict children's access to Internet sites.

A contrast is the Cuyahoga County Public Library. Its twenty-nine-branch service area overlaps the Cleveland system's. Teens and children need parental permission to use Internet terminals with pictures. First, the minor checks in with a staff member. Then, the staff member checks the consent forms on file.

The minor then gets a sticker that he or she must display while using the computer. Other terminals with text-only Internet access can be used without parental consent.[19]

Can young people view offensive sites in school computer laboratories? Many schools have students sign "acceptable-use policies." These usually restrict student use of school terminals to course-related work. Most students must also promise not to engage in destructive activities. These include sending viruses or harassing e-mail.[20]

So far, early cases suggest problems with filter use by libraries. Until there are more cases, the issue will remain open.

Meanwhile, library policies vary. Some have no restrictions; others require parental consent. Rules calling for parental consent should withstand court challenge.

Teen Web Sites

Thirteen-year-old Aaron Smith was not the world's greatest artist, but he enjoyed working on the computer. Then a friend joked that his computer laboratory drawing resembled a dying chihuahua. The remark became a standing joke.

Aaron went home and designed his own "CHOW" Web page. CHOW stood for "Chihuahua Haters of the World." Among other things, Aaron wrote a fake news report about a boa constrictor devouring a chihuahua. Aaron listed himself as the author. He also noted that he was a student at Dowell Middle School in McKinney, Texas.

A dog breeder in Fort Worth, Texas, complained to Aaron's school. Other animal lovers sent irate e-mail messages to the school superintendent.

School officials thought the page came from the computer lab. They suspended Aaron for a day and transferred him out of the lab. They also demanded that he remove the Web site and post an apology.[21]

"This was a bizarre intrusion on his free speech rights," declared ACLU staff writer Ann Beeson. The ACLU negotiated a legal settlement. Aaron got back into computer class. The school also agreed not to list the incident on Aaron's permanent record.[22]

Sean O'Brien disliked his Westlake High School band teacher. So he put the Ohio teacher's photo on his Web site. He called the teacher "an overweight middle-aged man who doesn't like to get haircuts." He also faulted the teacher for thinking "that problems are caused by a certain student or group of students and no one else."[23]

The school suspended Sean for eight days. It also threatened to expel him. In response, Sean sued the school district. He claimed the school violated his First Amendment rights.

Federal judge John Manos ordered the school to let Sean back into class.[24] Soon after, the school district paid thirty thousand dollars to settle Sean's claim.[25]

High school senior Paul Kim designed his Web site in Bellevue, Washington. It was a parody of his school newspaper. School officials told Paul they disliked

Acceptable use policies govern how teens use computers at school. Whether schools can regulate use at home is still being fought in the courts.

the site. Then they withdrew a recommendation for a National Merit Scholarship. If Paul had won, he could have gotten thousands of dollars for college. The ACLU took legal action on Paul's behalf and won a favorable money settlement.[26]

Brandon Beussink, a seventeen-year-old from Marble Hill, Missouri, used curse words and insults on his Web page to criticize his high school. When the school tried to punish Brandon, he sued. A federal judge issued a preliminary order to keep the school from punishing Brandon.[27]

"I think the school should practice what it teaches," Brandon said when the ruling was announced. "We study history and we study the Constitution, but the school doesn't seem to think that applies to them."[28]

Not all teen Internet use is harmless. In March 1998 Cloverdale High School in California suspended all school Internet access. Officials suspected that several students broke into government computer systems.[29] In July 1998 two Cloverdale teens pleaded guilty to breaking into the Pentagon's computer system.[30]

This and other cases of hacking—unauthorized computer access—pose serious security risks. Hacking is also expensive. Out-of-pocket losses caused by hackers were reported by 241 companies in 1997. The total topped $1.3 million.[31]

Other teens use the Internet for personal threats. In Statesboro, Georgia, a fifteen-year-old was arrested in December 1997. His Web site included a threat to shoot the high school principal. It also had a threat to kidnap the principal's seven-year-old daughter. Officials felt the boy's statements posed a real danger to the principal and his family.[32]

More recently, eleven students in Brimfield Township, Ohio, had a Gothic-themed Web site. "Goths" dress in black. They share an interest in fantasy and certain music.[33]

The students' school suspended them. Less than two weeks earlier, two other teens killed thirteen people and wounded more than twenty others during a four-hour siege at Columbine High School in Colorado. The teen shooters there had also maintained a Goth-themed Web site. Ohio school officials worried that students with a Goth Web site might pose a danger at their school.

The ACLU objected. It claimed the school was unfairly punishing the teens for crimes by others. A favorable settlement cleared the students' records.[34]

Wrapping Up

The First Amendment covers communication on the Internet. Early court cases have struck down government efforts to restrict access to offensive Internet materials. But the law is still developing. Other restrictions may well withstand challenges.

Teens can say pretty much what they want to on personal Web pages. However, Web sites cannot threaten violence. If they do, schools and the police can take action against teens.

Teens also cannot do hacking, send viruses, or take other destructive actions. These acts are crimes for both teens and adults.

7

Curfews, Malls, Jobs, and Cars

The fifteen-year-old teen did not think he had done anything wrong. But police in Medina, Ohio, pulled over the car in which he was riding. Because it was 10:11 P.M., however, the boy was brought to police headquarters. The police charged him with curfew violation.[1]

One night in San Diego, sixteen-year-old Asha sat with her boyfriend inside his car. The car was parked a few blocks from her house. A police officer pulled up. The officer did not care that Asha had her mother's permission to be out. It was after 10 P.M. He arrested the honor student. "I didn't know where my daughter was for hours," recalled Asha's mother.[2]

Keeping Teens off the Streets

The United States Conference of Mayors reports that, as of 1997, 276 cities had youth curfews.[3] Curfews are laws that make it a crime to be out on the streets at certain times.

Curfews can be confusing. Many laws stagger curfew time with age. Younger teens have stricter deadlines. Older teens can stay out later. Teens may not recall which specific deadline applies. An urban area can include dozens of individual cities. Each city can have different laws.[4]

In 1998, for example, two Bay Village, Ohio, boys were in Cleveland one night after 11 P.M. Police arrested them, even though the boys could stay out until 1 A.M. in their own city. "Their parents were upset that we were enforcing our curfew on them," said a Cleveland police officer.[5]

Violating curfew can be serious. In Cleveland, for example, teens must go to juvenile court. One potential penalty is doing forced community service. The law also lets the court fine parents up to one hundred dollars.[6] The fine is supposed to make sure that parents will have their teens come home on time in the future.

Critics like the American Civil Liberties Union (ACLU) say the laws are unfair because they presume that teens who stay out late are guilty.[7] "A curfew makes it a crime just to be out on the street," objected ACLU spokesperson Robert Plotkin.[8]

"We believe teen curfews infringe on young people's right to be on the public streets, to associate freely with their friends, and to travel," explained Lenora Lapidus of the New Jersey ACLU. "And we also believe that these curfews infringe on the parents' right to raise their children as they see fit."[9]

Cities adopt curfews to reduce crime. They hope that keeping teens off the street at night will help.

Do curfews work? Some people say yes. Half the cities in the United States Conference of Mayors' survey—cities that had used youth curfews for ten years—had lower crime rates. In Cleveland, Ohio, police claim that curfews, plus community policing and other measures, reduced crime by 17 percent from 1990 through 1997.[10]

But curfews do not always help. To begin with, enforcement takes money and time. During one six-month period in 1997, Los Angeles police officers spent more than thirty-six hundred hours of police time issuing about forty-eight hundred youth curfew citations.[11]

A Justice Policy Institute study compared youth arrest rates among California cities with and without curfew laws. It found no decrease in arrests for the counties with curfews.[12]

Curfew supporters, such as Monrovia, California, police chief Joseph Santoro, said the study's statistics are biased. Arrest rates do not necessarily mean a real crime increase. Rather, they can show aggressive

Local curfew laws may regulate how late teens can stay out without parental supervision.

enforcement.[13] "Clearly, the commitment to strictly enforce the lesser offenses like curfews and truancies is discouraging youths from graduating into serious crimes," observed former California attorney general Dan Lungren.[14]

Another aim of curfew laws is to reduce school truancy. In 1997 seventy-six cities had daytime curfews for this purpose.[15] Officials in Monrovia, California, said their daytime curfew was helping cut school truancies by 39 percent. That is the equivalent of six thousand more school days attended by students in the city.[16]

Are curfews constitutional? That depends. Curfews are criminal laws. They must be clear and specific about their requirements. If a criminal law is too vague, it is unconstitutional.

Additionally, curfew laws must be narrow. Otherwise, they interfere with parents' rights and normal teen activities.

In 1999 a Los Angeles judge struck down the curfew for Monrovia, California. Despite the benefits claimed by supporters, the court found that the law was too restrictive.[17]

In 1997 a Washington State court ruled that Bellingham's curfew law was too vague. The law banned people under sixteen from being in any public place in the city's business district after 10 P.M. Sunday through Thursday. Curfew time was 11 P.M. on Friday and Saturday.[18]

"The number of juveniles engaged in safe and innocent activity almost certainly outnumbers those engaged in criminal activity," the court observed.[19] The city did not prove that the law's strict provisions were needed to address juvenile crime.

Teen Tiana Hutchins and other residents also brought a curfew challenge in Washington, D.C.[20] The city's law banned teens under seventeen from being in public places after 11 P.M. on weekdays and midnight on weekends.

"It is unfair to punish good kids who are out trying to make something of themselves when only a small percentage of young people are committing crimes in the city during curfew hours,"[21] said Tiana. The trial court ruled that the law was unconstitutional. In 1999, however, the appeals court decided to uphold the law.[22]

Another federal court upheld the curfew in Charlottesville, North Carolina.[23] The law had many exceptions. It did not apply if a parent was with a child. It did not cover errands run for the parent. It also did not apply to employment, interstate travel, supervised school and religious activities, and emergencies.

The teen challengers still objected. Because of the curfew, they could not go to late movies without their parents. They could not go out to eat after curfew hours. They could not go to concerts in other cities if they would get home after curfew.

In *Schleifer* v. *City of Charlottesville*, the court ruled that the law "comfortably satisfies" constitutional requirements. "The Charlottesville curfew serves not only to head off crimes before they occur," the court wrote, "but also to protect a particularly vulnerable population from being lured into participating in such activity."[24]

Thus, courts have gone both ways on the issue of curfews. Narrow laws, like the Charlottesville curfew, are more likely to withstand challenge. Such laws have many exceptions. They try to achieve a goal—lower crime rates—with the least interference.

Other curfew laws have been held unconstitutional. Laws such as that from Washington, D.C., have fewer exceptions. They reach too broadly. They try to reduce crime but restrict teen freedom too much. Vague language can also doom a curfew law.

In any case, teens should know whether their city has a curfew. They should also know what it provides. Curfews can be confusing, so teens should direct any questions to their local police department or city council.

At the Mall

Minnesota's giant Mall of America hosts thousands of shoppers each day. On Friday and Saturday evenings, though, anyone under age sixteen must be with an adult over age twenty-one.[25] This private curfew is the mall's Parental Escort Policy.

Stores cannot lawfully discriminate against customers on the basis of gender, race, or religion. However, private businesses can generally restrict how and if they will do business with minors.

Before Mall of America's policy went into effect in 1996, about five thousand teens visited the mall each weekend night.[26] Teens could shop at more than four hundred stores. They could visit the 4.2-million-square-foot mall's movie theaters. They could go to a miniature golf course, amusement park, and aquarium.

Most teens behaved, but fights did break out. One teen even brandished a gun at a tourist in a food court. "We knew the best thing to do was to have more supervision, so we decided to go with this," said Mall of America's assistant general manager Maureen Bausch.[27]

Slick signs styled like movie posters announced the mall was now "rated 16." "You Can't Go Alone," the signs told younger teens.[28] But some younger shoppers were still upset. "They just took away the best shopping days," said fourteen-year-old Jackie Soucek.[29]

The first weekend that the new policy was in effect, Mall of America attendance stayed at about the one hundred thousand mark. But there were no fights.[30] As this book goes to press, the policy is still in effect.

"It's phenomenal," said Wendy Williams, Mall of America's director of marketing. "We had over three hundred arrests the year before we had Parental Escort." The following year, there was only one arrest. "It's a completely different atmosphere on weekend nights," said Williams.[31]

Some bowling alleys and other businesses only let teens enter without adult supervision at certain times. The Mall of America has advised other malls on how to adopt similar policies.[32] "You need to have

Welcome to Mall of America
A Smoke Free Property

In order to assist in our efforts to provide a safe, secure and pleasant shopping environment, we ask for your cooperation with the following:

- Conduct that is disorderly, disruptive or which interferes with or endangers business or guests is prohibited. Such conduct may include running, loud, offensive language, spitting, throwing objects, fighting, obscene gestures, etc.
- Loitering, blocking storefronts, hallways, skyways, fire exits or escalators, and walking in groups in such a way as to inconvenience others is prohibited.
- The commission of any act defined by Federal, State or local ordinances as a criminal act is prohibited, such as carrying weapons, grafitti or property damage, etc.
- Picketing, demonstrating, distributing handbills, soliciting and petitioning require the prior written consent of mall management.
- Appropriate non-offensive attire, including shirts and shoes, must be worn.
- Only pets trained to assist persons with disabilities are permitted within the mall.
- General Cinema guests under 16 may enter through the South Avenue Level One Entrance without a parent or guardian on Fridays and Saturdays 6:00 pm to close.

All violators will be asked to leave the property or possibly arrested.

Parental Escort Policy
We welcome all youths to Mall of America, but on Friday and Saturday evenings youths under 16 must be accompanied by an adult 21 years or older from 6:00 p.m. until closing. One adult may supervise up to 10 youth. Anyone 21 years or younger should be prepared to show a driver's license, state identification card, passport or Mall employee identification card during the Parental Escort hours.

To obtain a Minnesota State Identification Card, contact your local driver exam or driver license renewal office, or call 612-296-6911. The cost is $12.50.

MALL OF AMERICA.

A welcome sign at Minnesota's Mall of America advises shoppers of the mall's parental escort policy.

a very specific plan laid out," explained Williams.[33] Most malls, in fact, want young shoppers, but they also want to make sure that the malls remain safe for all shoppers.

Malls, bowling alleys, and stores are private businesses. They have a legal right to deal with minors only at certain times or to require adult supervision. Such policies can and do restrict teen rights. Teens who do not like the policies can choose to shop elsewhere. Indeed, teens spent $122 billion in 1997.[34] That is a lot of money that many stores want to attract.

Teens on the Job

Part-time jobs make teens a significant part of the workforce. American teens earned almost $111 billion in 1997.[35]

Federal and state laws regulate where and when teens can work. They also control how much teens can earn.

Labor laws for minors were a long time in coming. In colonial times, children on farms had to work the family's fields. City children learned trades. They worked as apprentices for other family businesses.

The Industrial Revolution brought more factories to America. Companies needed cheap labor. Children often worked for cheaper wages than adults. And many families desperately needed what little money the children earned.

Until almost the mid–twentieth century, factory workers had to labor long hours. Conditions were often unsanitary and unsafe. In 1911 a fire broke out at New York's Triangle Shirtwaist Company. Getting to the only fire escape required climbing through a tiny window. The fire killed one hundred forty workers. Many were young boys and girls.[36]

The Triangle factory fire did not change the law. But it led to public outcry about oppressive working conditions. Child rights advocates called for laws to protect workers.

Finally, in 1938 Congress passed the Fair Labor Standards Act.[37] It banned employment of minors under sixteen years of age in various industries. It also said that teens under eighteen could not hold jobs in certain industries, such as mining and logging.[38] These jobs present unusually hazardous working conditions.

The law also set a minimum hourly wage.[39] Congress has raised the minimum wage at various times.[40] All workers, including teens, must earn at least that much, unless an exception applies. Restaurant servers who get tips, for example, may get paid less than the federal minimum wage.

Generally, minors who want to work need a work permit. Most school districts can issue the permits. In Ohio, for example, teens must submit a description of the proposed job, a statement from their doctor that they can do the work, parental consent, and a statement of the employer's intention to comply with labor laws. Federal and state laws limit how many hours a minor can work each day and week, particularly during the school year.

Teens work hard for their money. While parents can sometimes apply teens' wages toward the cost of necessities, most parents and teens make an arrangement for part-time job earnings that they consider fair.

Many employers comply with labor laws. But the law has loopholes.

Approximately one million children and teens work in agriculture. Many are migrant farmworkers. They travel with their families from farm to farm and are paid according to how much they harvest.[41]

Exemptions in federal law let farms hire child workers as young as ten years old if they can show that not using children would disrupt the industry.[42] The children's work conditions are often oppressive.[43] Many work twelve to fourteen hours each day.[44] Some use tools, drive tractors and trucks, or work around mechanical equipment. Others are exposed to chemical pesticides. About twenty thousand injuries occur among underage farmworkers each year.[45]

Even when labor laws do apply, some employers may break the law. For example, some stores have teens work longer hours than federal and state laws allow.[46]

Not all teens feel that they need the protection of child labor laws. Fourteen-year-old Tommy McCoy became angry when the Georgia labor department got him fired from his dream job. Tommy was a bat boy for the Savannah Cardinals' baseball farm team.

Because of the time and length of games, Tommy worked more hours per day than the law allowed. When the matter became public, the Department of Labor granted an exemption from the law. Soon after, the law was changed to let other "underage" teens work for their favorite teams.[47]

What do teens do with their paychecks? Technically, the money belongs to them. But parents have limited rights to the money. They can use it to pay for some of the necessities they must provide by law.[48]

Also, when minors earn huge amounts (either as athletes or entertainers), wages may have to go into trust funds. If parents mismanage the money, courts can name another trustee. In New York, for example, teen actor Macaulay Culkin objected to his father's financial management. A New York judge reviewed the case. Then, instead of the father, he appointed an accountant to oversee Culkin's trust fund.[49]

Most teens do not earn such huge amounts. In 1997 average weekly earnings were about eighty dollars for teens aged sixteen and seventeen.[50] Because this is not a large amount, court cases are rare.

Most teens control their own wages. Clothing is their biggest expense.[51] Entertainment and food rank second and third.[52]

Despite small individual earnings, teens as a group earn a lot of money. When teens work, they are entitled to protection under federal and state labor laws. The laws limit how long teens can work and which jobs they can do.

Teen workers deserve the same protections as other workers. Employers must protect them against injuries. They cannot discriminate on the basis of race, religion, or gender. And in most cases, they must pay minimum wage.

Teens who have any questions or concerns can contact the nearest office of the Department of Labor or their state labor departments. The agencies can take action against any employer who violates labor laws.

On the Road

Laws on teen driving vary from state to state. Some states require teens first to get a learner's permit or junior license. Other states require minors to take driver education before they can get a license. Still others limit the times that teen drivers can be on the road. Teens can check with their state motor vehicle departments on specific rules that apply to them.

Almost all states have compulsory insurance laws. These laws say all drivers must have liability insurance. Driving without such insurance can mean losing one's driver's license.[53]

Drunk driving is an offense in all fifty states and the District of Columbia. Legal limits for intoxication vary from state to state for adults. By the end of 1998, however, all states were required to adopt near zero-tolerance laws for drivers under age twenty-one. If even one drink's worth of alcohol is detected, a young driver can be convicted.[54]

Wrapping Up

Outside of home and school, teens may find themselves subject to restrictions because of their age. Curfews make it against the law for young people to be on the streets at certain times.

Some curfews are constitutional, but others may not be. Deciding factors include how specific the law is and what exceptions are allowed.

Private businesses may restrict how and when they deal with teens. As long as the rules are not based on race, gender, or religion, they are likely to be held valid.

Teens also are subject to rules when they get part-time jobs. Federal law restricts how long teens can work each day and sets a minimum wage. State laws can also apply.

Many teens look forward to the privilege of driving. Licensing laws and insurance requirements vary from state to state.

8

In Court

Laws on youth crime have changed with time. In colonial times, laws were very harsh.

In the Massachusetts Bay Colony, the Puritans punished children over age seven as if they were adults. One 1646 "stubborn child" law even had the death penalty as a possible punishment. It applied if teens over age sixteen cursed or struck their parents.[1]

By the nineteenth century, many people felt the laws were too harsh. Children's rights advocates argued that minors were not like hardened criminals. Rather, they said, young people could be rehabilitated (returned to good behavior as useful society members).

Rehabilitation assumed that young people could still learn how to act properly. This was nearly impossible, however, in a system that lumped adult and youth offenders together.

Juvenile Justice

Slowly, cities began setting up separate prisons for young offenders.[2] Minors were still tried in adult courts. They were still sentenced as if they were adults. But they were kept away from older, hardened criminals.

In 1899, Illinois set up the Cook County Juvenile Court. It was the United States' first juvenile court.[3]

The new court could take whatever action it felt was in the child's best interests. It could remove children under sixteen from their homes and send them to institutions. Or it could place them on probation.

Other states soon followed suit. The goal was not punishment. Thus, juvenile court cases were not called "criminal" matters. Hearings were informal and private to keep youths from being branded as criminals. Today, all states and the District of Columbia have a juvenile court system.

These informal courts aimed to help young people who broke the law. However, the system failed to teach skills to avoid getting in trouble again. Many offenders returned again and again to treatment centers or reform schools.

Juvenile courts were not supposed to punish children, but they could still be harsh. Some minors went to institutions for longer than they would have gone to jail if they were adults.

More important, until the 1960s minors did not get the same rights as adults. Adults had due process rights guaranteed by the Constitution. Juvenile courts often denied these basic rights.

Gerald Gault discovered this unfairness first-hand. In 1964 police officers claimed that Gerald made an obscene phone call. No attorney represented him in juvenile court, and the woman accusing Gerald did not testify under oath in court. Indeed, no one ever proved that Gerald in fact made the call.[4]

Going to juvenile court can be scary for a teen. This building houses the juvenile court for Cuyahoga County, Ohio.

If Gerald were an adult, the maximum sentence would have been two months in jail, a fifty dollar fine, or both. However, Arizona juvenile judge Robert McGhee ruled that fifteen-year-old Gerald was a "delinquent child." He ordered Gerald to go to the state's juvenile delinquent home. Gerald could have been kept there until his twenty-first birthday.[5]

The juvenile court found Gerald guilty. It sentenced him to up to six years for allegedly making one obscene phone call.

Gerald served six months at Arizona's "industrial school."[6] It was really an institution for juvenile offenders. Meanwhile, his parents appealed to the Supreme Court.

"Neither the Fourteenth Amendment nor the Bill of Rights is for adults alone," wrote Supreme Court Justice Abe Fortas in *In re Gault*.[7] Minors such as Gerald deserve due process rights.

First, minors need timely notice of charges and hearings. This lets them prepare a defense. Due process also includes the right to counsel. This means that minors can have an attorney. Attorneys know how the courts work. They are trained to represent clients effectively.

Due process also includes the right against self-incrimination. Courts cannot force a minor to testify against him- or herself. And the police cannot force minors to confess.

Minors also have the right to have their lawyers cross-examine witnesses. Cross-examination lets lawyers spotlight flaws in a witness's story. For example, a witness might not be sure what happened. Or the witness might have some bias. Bias can make the testimony unreliable.

The Supreme Court expanded young people's rights further in *In re Winship*.[8] The police charged twelve-year-old Samuel Winship with larceny, or property theft. A saleswoman identified Samuel as a boy she had seen running away shortly after noticing that money was missing from her store.[9]

The New York family court judge held a hearing. He listened to the saleswoman. He also heard testimony from Samuel's family, who said he had been home at the time. The judge decided the saleswoman's statements were more believable. He ruled that Samuel was delinquent by a preponderance of the evidence.[10]

A preponderance of the evidence means that something is more likely to be true than not. It is a much lower standard than proof beyond a reasonable doubt—the standard that applies in adult criminal cases. Samuel's lawyers appealed the case all the way to the Supreme Court.

The Supreme Court ruled that young people are entitled to have the standard of proof beyond a reasonable doubt. In other words, it gave young defendants the benefit of the same high burden of proof that adults have.[11]

Because of *In re Gault, In re Winship*, and other cases, young people now enjoy constitutional protections when they are charged with crimes. They also have their own justice system. Juvenile courts are supposed to meet the needs of young offenders.

Problems still sometimes occur, though. At

Arizona's Catalina Mountain Juvenile Institution, seventeen-year-old Matt Johnson sat in solitary confinement for more than seven weeks. Officials said Matt threatened a staff member, but they did not prove the claim. For those seven weeks, Matt had no educational, psychological, or recreational programming. He had no idea when his punishment would end. Matt could do nothing on his own, so his father filed a lawsuit.[12]

Seven years later, the court entered a consent decree in *Johnson* v. *Upchurch*.[13] The facility had to change its practices and eliminate overcrowding.

But problems continued. In February 1997, the court held the state in contempt. Arizona later made changes.[14]

Johnson was an unusual case. Most states do better at running detention centers for teens. But teens and parents may still have to take action to enforce their rights. States owe teens due process—both before and after any finding of guilt.

For First-Time Offenders

Some states have developed alternatives to sending teens to prison.

During the 1980s, Odessa and other Texas cities popularized teen courts. These are juvenile justice courts run for teens by teens. By 1998, 560 cities and counties in 46 states plus the District of Columbia had teen courts.[15]

Teen court programs vary. Most are limited to first-time offenders. Almost all teen court programs apply only to misdemeanors. In most states, a misdemeanor is a crime that can be punished by less than one year in prison. Typical examples include curfew violations, trespassing, and shoplifting.

Almost all programs require the accused teen to admit guilt. The offender must also give up the right to an attorney. Then the teen court holds a sentencing hearing.

Using teen courts means giving up some due process rights. That is fine for teens who admit guilt. Teens who say they are innocent must still use traditional juvenile court systems. They must press for their due process rights.

Usually, a teen prosecutor argues for a strict

Teens can learn to stand up for their rights and for each other.

sentence. Then a teen defender argues for something less strict. Teen jurors confer with each other. Then they render a verdict.

Typical sentences involve supervised community service. Most offenders must also write apologies and pay for anything taken or damaged. Counseling and educational activities also form part of the typical sentence package.[16]

Offenders must also return to serve with other teens on a future case. They act as jurors and help sentence other offenders. After the teen completes all parts of the sentence, charges are dismissed. The teen offender has no criminal record.[17]

"We refer to our youths as good kids who've made bad choices," explains Lolita Junk, who has served as staff coordinator for the Knox County Teen Court in Illinois.[18] "They learn to assume responsibility and to learn accountability for their actions," says Junk, "which is something that doesn't happen if they're just given a slap on the wrist and if Mom and Dad pay a fine." While nationwide statistics are not available, the Knox County program boasts a 90 percent success rate.[19]

Teen courts provide a good choice for young people who have broken the law. They can make amends without getting a criminal record.

Acts of Violence

At the other end of the spectrum are violent teen crimes. In certain cases, teens can lose their rights to special treatment as youthful offenders.

When the fire alarm rang shortly after lunch at a Jonesboro, Arkansas, middle school, students and teachers filed out into the school yard. Suddenly, bullets flew everywhere, hitting fifteen people. Five victims died, including four girls and sixth-grade teacher Shannon Wright. Police arrested thirteen-year-old Mitchell Johnson and eleven-year-old Andrew Golden, charging them with the slayings.[20]

If an adult had committed the Jonesboro murders, he or she could have gotten the death penalty. Or an adult shooter might have gotten life in prison.

In 1998, however, both boys were under age fourteen. They were too young to be tried as adults under existing Arkansas law. Instead, they could only be sent to a juvenile detention facility until their twenty-first birthdays.

Both boys got this maximum sentence, but many people felt it was woefully inadequate. "The punishment will not fit the crime," said Judge Wilson as he gave the sentence. The victims' families held each other and cried.[21]

Sadly, these were not the first teens to commit murder. But the murders shocked people because they occurred in a suburban, middle-class area. The murders made national headlines. Together with other cases of school violence, they sparked debate. Are existing juvenile justice laws too lenient?

Every state and the District of Columbia now has at least one law allowing juvenile offenders to be tried as adults in some cases. As of 1998, the District of Columbia and twenty-one states had no minimum age below which a child could be tried as an adult if certain facts applied. Minimum ages for being tried as an adult in the remaining states ranged from sixteen down to seven.[22]

In New York, for example, police charged sixteen-year-old Brian Wright as an adult. Wright allegedly shot a twelve-year-old boy in a dispute over a quarter. "This was a senseless, mindless killing,"[23] said Richard Brown, the Queens district attorney in charge of the case.

In Oregon, officials prosecuted fifteen-year-old Kip Kinkel as an adult on the charge that Kinkel killed his parents and shot twenty-four students at Thurston High School.[24] Kinkel was sentenced to life in prison.

And in Mississippi, seventeen-year-old Luke Woodham was sentenced to life in prison. He allegedly stabbed and beat his mother. Then, police charged, Woodham went on a shooting spree, killing a former girlfriend and her friend.[25]

These and other cases suggest that teen rights are slowly being replaced by adult punishments. When school violence makes headlines, people demand action.[26]

After school shootings killed twelve people at Columbine High School in Colorado, many schools announced zero-tolerance policies. Schools would charge students making threats with violating school rules, and would call the police at any threat of violence.

Both schools and the police want to protect teens from violence. It is not yet clear how reactions to school shootings will affect teen rights. For serious crimes, the pendulum seems to be swinging toward treating young offenders more harshly.

Wrapping Up

The United States Constitution guarantees due process and other rights to minors accused of crimes. Minors cannot be forced to incriminate themselves. They have the right to a lawyer. They have the right to know the charges against them. They have the right to require witnesses to testify under oath. And they have the right to have guilt proved beyond a reasonable doubt. Basically, juvenile offenders now have much the same protections as adult defendants.

Most young offenders are tried by juvenile courts rather than by adult criminal courts. Some cities and counties use alternative programs such as teen courts for nonviolent first offenses. At the other end of the spectrum, teens who commit violent crimes are sometimes tried and sentenced as adults.

Teens need to know and understand their rights in order to stand up for themselves. Sometimes teens have the same rights as adults. Sometimes they have more protections. And sometimes teens must deal with more restrictions.

Other people do not always automatically respect the rights of teens. So teens need to ask questions and assert their rights.

Some rights vary from state to state. An example is the right to consent to medical treatment without parental input. Teens can talk to a doctor, contact a local board of health, or call a medical clinic to learn about their own state's laws.

Federal and state law is constantly evolving. Changes over time reflect young people's changing roles in society.

Teens can protect their rights by learning effective communication methods. For example, a teen may feel that a teacher treats him or her unfairly. It may be tempting to shout, "You can't do that to me!" But a request to meet with the teacher, along with a parent and administrator, can be more effective.

If a teen's own efforts to assert his or her legal rights fail, the teen can turn to the courts. Outside help is sometimes available. The American Civil Liberties Union and National Student Law Center have helped many young people take their cases to court. These groups usually get involved only when a constitutional issue is at stake, such as freedom of speech or due process.

Without help from such groups, litigation can be costly and time consuming. Enough has to be at stake to make a lawsuit worth it. But if a substantial injury has occurred, legal action may be justified.

Finally, teens should also respect the rights of fellow teens. Harassment at school, for example, hurts everybody. Concerned teens can tell offenders to stop or notify school administrators. Promoting an atmosphere in which all teens are protected helps ensure that everyone's rights are preserved.

Where to Go for Help

American Civil Liberties Union
125 Broad St., 18th Floor
New York, NY 10004
(212) 549-2500
<http://www.aclu.org>

Children's Defense Fund
25 E St. NW
Washington, DC 20001
(202) 628-8787
<http://www.childrensdefense.org>

National Center for Youth Law
114 Sansome St., Suite 900
San Francisco, CA 94104
(415) 543-3307
<http://www.youthlaw.org>

National Committee to Prevent Child Abuse
200 S. Michigan Ave.
Chicago, IL 60604
(312) 663-3520
<http://www.childabuse.com>

Student Law Press Center
1815 N. Fort Myer Drive, Suite 900
Arlington, Virginia 22209
(703) 807-1904
<http://www.splc.org>

Local Organizations
Consult your local telephone directory under government listings to locate your board of health or department of social services and child welfare.

Chapter Notes

Chapter 1. Everyone Has Rights—Right?

1. Dominique Moceanu, as told to Steve Woodward, *Dominique Moceanu, An American Champion: An Autobiography* (New York: Bantam, 1996), p. 13.

2. Ibid.

3. Pam Lambert, "Settling a Fight for Control of Her Future, an Olympic Gymnast Makes Peace With Her Parents," *People Weekly*, November 9, 1998, p. 55.

4. Kendall Hamilton, "A Very Ugly Gym Suit," *Newsweek*, November 2, 1998, p. 52.

5. Jere Longman, "Moceanu Gets Adult Status in Dispute Over Her Money," *The New York Times*, October 29, 1998, p. D4.

6. "The Moceanu Case: Whose Money Is It, Anyway?" *Sports Illustrated*, November 2, 1998, p. 40.

7. Sharon Raboin, "Moceanu Gets Right to Control Her Career," *USA Today*, October 29, 1998, p. 6C.

8. Jere Longman, "Moceanu Gets Protective Order," *The New York Times*, December 1, 1998, p. D1.

9. E. M. Swift, "Daddy Dearest," *Sports Illustrated*, December 21, 1998, p. 101.

10. Ibid.; "Dominique Moceanu," *U.S. News & World Report*, December 21, 1998, p. 16; Longman, p. D1.

11. Frank Litsky, "Olympic Champion Settles Dispute with Her Father," *The New York Times*, April 10, 1999, p. D2.

12. *Parham* v. *J. R.*, 422 U.S. 584, 602–03 (1979).

13. Ibid.

14. Fair Labor Standards Act, 29 U.S.C. 201 et seq.

15. Catherine Elton, "Jail Baiting," *New Republic*, October 20, 1997, p. 12.

16. See *In re T. A. J.*, California Court of Appeals, First Appellate District, Div. 2, April 9, 1998, <http://law.miningco.com/library/blminors.htm> (August 23, 1999).

17. Arnold Beichman, "Statutory Rape Laws Must Be Enforced," *Insight on the News*, May 13, 1996, p. 30.

18. Marie McCullough, "Advocates of Statutory-Rape Crackdown Say Tougher Laws Will Reduce Teen Pregnancy," Knight-Ridder/Tribune News Service, April 4, 1997, p. 404K47757; Stephanie Goldberg, "Jailbait: Politicians Dust off Old Sex Laws to Combat Teenage Pregnancy," *Playboy*, January 1997, p. 41.

19. Margaret Jasper, *Juvenile Justice and Children's Law* (Dobbs Ferry, N.Y.: Oceana Publications, Inc., 1994), pp. 3–5.

20. Joseph M. Hawes, *The Children's Rights Movement: A History of Advocacy and Protection* (Boston: Twayne Publishers, 1991), pp. 99–105.

21. Michael Simpson, "Prayer in Schools: What the Law Allows," *NEA Today*, October 1995, p. 25.

22. Perry Glanzer, "Religion in Public Schools: In Search of Fairness," *Phi Delta Kappan*, November 1998, p. 219; Arthur Jones, "Clinton: OK to Pray if It's Private, Outside Class," *National Catholic Reporter*, July 28, 1995, p. 5.

Chapter 2. Teen Rights at Home

1. Joseph M. Hawes, *The Children's Rights Movement: A History of Advocacy and Protection* (Boston: Twayne Publishers, 1991), pp. 1–4.

2. K. M. Kowalski, "I Need Some Privacy!" *Current Health 2*, October 1996, p. 16; Andrea Thompson, "Kids & Privacy: The 6 Hot Spots," *Good Housekeeping*, May 1995, p. 168.

3. Peter Stevens and Marian Eide, "The First Chapter of Children's Rights," *American Heritage*, July/August 1990, p. 84.

4. Ibid.

5. Jack Westman, ed., *Who Speaks for the Children: The Handbook of Individual and Child Class Advocacy* (Sarasota, Fla.: Professional Resource Exchange, Inc., 1991), pp. 210–211.

6. Beverly Edmonds and William Fernekes, *Children's Rights: A Reference Handbook* (Santa Barbara, Calif.: ABC-CLIO, 1996), pp. 237–262.

7. National Committee to Prevent Child Abuse, "Child Abuse and Neglect Statistics," April 1998, <http://www.childabuse.org/facts97.html> (August 23, 1999).

8. Ibid.

9. Ibid.

10. Stephen Flynn, "Director's Corner," *Family Matters*, Fall 1998, p. 1.

11. Westman, pp. 211–219, 253–254.

12. National Children's Coalition, "Street Kids and Runaway Youth," 1998 <http://www.child.net/runaway.htm> (August 23, 1999).

13. Jane Gross, "Fleeing Abuse to the Streets," *The New York Times*, December 18, 1997, p. B1.

14. Sarah Tippert, "I've Got the Family I Always Wanted," *Ladies Home Journal*, April 1993, p. 150.

15. Pat Wingert and Eloise Salholz, "Irreconcilable Differences," *Newsweek,* September 21, 1992, pp. 84–85.

16. "A Child Asserts His Legal Rights," *Time*, October 5, 1992, p. 22.

17. "The Home of His Choice," *People Weekly*, October 12, 1992, p. 57.

18. Jean Seligman, "Stirring Up the Muddy Waters," *Newsweek*, August 30, 1993, p. 58.

19. Peter Mitchell, "Florida Baby-Swap Suit Goes to Trial," Knight-Ridder/Tribune News Service, August 2, 1993, p. 0802K5321.

20. Steve Fishman, "Breaking the Silence," *Vogue*, March 1997, p. 342.

21. Ibid.

22. Kevin Gray, "A Need to Be Heard," *People Weekly*, June 26, 1995, p. 48.

23. Michael G. MacDonald et al., eds., *Treatise on Health Care Law*, vol. 3 (New York: Matthew Bender, 1998), §19.03[3][6].

Chapter 3. Teens and Their Bodies

1. Michael G. MacDonald et al., eds., *Treatise on Health Care Law*, vol. 3 (New York: Matthew Bender, 1998), §§19.02—19.03.

2. *Lundman* v. *McKown*, 530 N.W. 2d 807 (Minn. 1995), cert. denied 116 S.Ct. 814 (1996).

3. Mark Larabee, "Faith vs. Medicine," *Cleveland Plain Dealer*, January 9, 1999, p. 1F.

4. Telephone interview with Abigail English, December 21, 1998.

5. As of 1993, over twenty states followed some form of the mature minor doctrine; "Consent for Medical Services for Children and Adolescents (RE9309)," *Pediatrics*, August 1993, p. 290.

6. MacDonald, §19.01[4].

7. Patricia Booth Levenberg, "Ensuring Confidentiality Important in Treating Teens," *American Medical News*, October 7, 1996, p. 34.

8. MacDonald, §19.03[1].

9. Personal interview with Anne Safrath, December 29, 1998.

10. Telephone interview with Abigail English.

11. *"Consent for Medical Services for Children and Adolescents,"* p. 290.

12. MacDonald, §19.01[3][b].

13. American Academy of Pediatrics, press release, "Declines in Teen Pregnancy and Abortion Rates," November 2, 1998; Deborah Forman, *Every Parent's Guide to the Law* (New York: Harcourt Brace, 1998), p. 137.

14. MacDonald, §19.01[3][a].

15. Roger J. R. Levesque, "The Peculiar Place of Adolescents in the HIV/AIDS Epidemic: Unusual Progress & Usual Inadequacies in 'Adolescent Jurisprudence,'" *Loyola University Chicago Law Journal*, 1996, p. 232.

16. Telephone interview with Abigail English.

17. "The Adolescent's Right to Confidential Care When Considering Abortion (RE9614)," *Pediatrics*, May 1996, p. 746.

18. Deborah L. Forman, *Every Parent's Guide to the Law* (Orlando, Fla.: Harcourt Brace & Co., 1989), p. 144.

19. Ibid.

20. *Roe* v. *Wade*, 410 U.S. 113 (1973).

21. Marcia Henry, "California High Court Rejects Parental Consent for Abortion Law," *Youth Law News*, July/August 1997, p. 4.

22. Telephone interview with Abigail English.

23. *Ohio* v. *Akron Center for Reproductive Health*, 497 U.S. 502 (1990); *Hodgson* v. *Minnesota*, 497 U.S. 417 (1990). State constitutions may also affect parental consent laws. See *American Academy of Pediatrics* v. *Lungren*, 66 Cal.Rptr.2d 210 (1997).

24. Telephone interview with Abigail English.

25. Holly Metz, "Branding Juveniles Against Their Will," *Student Lawyer*, February 1992, p. 22.

26. *Parham* v. *J.R.*, 442 U.S. 584 (1979); see also *Bartley* v. *Kremens*, 424 U.S. 964 (1976).

27. Joan-Margaret Kun, "Rejecting the Adage 'Children Should Be Seen and Not Heard'—The Mature Minor Doctrine," *Pace Law Review*, 1996, p. 423.

28. Ibid., p. 424.

29. "Informed Consent, Parental Permission, and Assent in Pediatric Practice (RE9510)," *Pediatrics*, February 1995, p. 314.

30. *Novak* v. *Cobb County Kennestone Hospital Authority*, 74 F.3d 1173 (11th Cir., 1996).

31. Gail B. Slap and Martha Jablow, "Debating the Rights of Young Patients," *The New York Times*, November 10, 1994, p. C10.

32. Rebecca Voelker, "Ryan White, 18, Dies After 5-Year Battle with AIDS," *American Medical News*, April 20, 1990, p. 11; Jack Friedman, "The Quiet Victories of Ryan White," *People Weekly*, May 30, 1988, p. 88.

33. Louis Fischer et al., *Teachers and the Law*, 4th ed. (White Plains, N.Y.: Longman Publishers, 1995), pp. 102–110.

34. Fischer et al., pp. 107–110.

35. Title IX, Education Amendments of 1972, 20 U.S.C. 1681 et seq.

36. "Teen Pregnancy Getting Caught," *Virginian-Pilot*, December 2, 1998, p. B8; Vivian Martin, "Teen Pregnancy a Victim of Generation Gap," *Hartford Courant*, August 13, 1998, p. A23.

37. "The Scarlet 'P'," *St. Louis Post-Dispatch*, August 15, 1998, p. 34.

38. *Chipman* v. *Grant County School Dist.*, No. 98–200 (E.D. Ky., December 30, 1998); ACLU, press release, "Kentucky Court Says Teen Moms Must Be Admitted Into National Honor Society," December 30, 1998.

Chapter 4. The Rules at School

1. Stefanie Weiss, "Flirting or Hurting?" *NEA Today*, April 1994, p. 4.

2. Tony Mauro, "Will Every Childish Taunt Turn Into a Federal Case?" *USA Today*, May 25, 1999, p. 1A.

3. *Davis* v. *Monroe County Board of Education*, United States Supreme Court, No. 97–843, May 24, 1999.

4. Buckley Amendment to Family Educational Rights and Privacy Act of 1974, 20 U.S.C. 1232g.

5. Ibid.

6. Louis Fischer et al., *Teachers and the Law*, 4th ed. (White Plains, N.Y.: Longman Publishers, 1995), p. 397; 68 American Jurisprudence 2d, Schools, §§228–240 (Rochester, N.Y.: Lawyers Cooperative, 1993 and 1998 supplement).

7. Wisconsin v. Yoder, 406 U.S. 205 (1972).

8. Scott Baldauf, "Graduation Requirement: Good Deeds," *Christian Science Monitor*, February 19, 1997, p. 12.

9. Kevin Johnson, "Schools Force Students to Learn Value of Service," *USA Today*, May 4, 1998, p. 6D.

10. Baldauf, "Graduation Requirement," p. 12.

11. Scott Baldauf, "Mandatory Community Service Withstands Legal Challenge," *Christian Science Monitor*, February 24, 1997, p. 12.

12. Perry Zirkel, "The Midol Case," *Phi Delta Kappan*, June 1997, p. 803.

13. *Goss* v. *Lopez*, 419 U.S. 565 (1975).

14. Ibid.

15. Ibid.

16. *C. B.* v. *Driscoll*, 82 F.3d 383 (11th Cir. 1996).

17. *Ingraham* v. *Wright*, 430 U.S. 651 (1977).

18. Fischer et al., *Teachers and the Law*, pp. 264–265.

19. *P. B.* v. *Koch*, 96 F.3d 1298 (9th Cir. 1996).

20. *Wallace* v. *Batavia School Dist.* 101, 68 F.3d 1010, 1016 (7th Cir. 1995).

21. Fischer et al., *Teachers and the Law*, pp. 261–262.

22. *New Jersey* v. *T. L. O.*, 469 U.S. 325 (1985).

23. Ibid.

24. *Smith* v. *McGlothlin*, 119 F.3d 786 (9th Cir. 1997).

25. Telephone interview with Kent Willis, Executive Director for ACLU of Virginia, November 12, 1999; American Civil Liberties Union, press release, "Student Privacy Rights Go on Trial in Virginia," April 27, 1998.

26. American Civil Liberties Union, press release, "Student Strip Searches: Lawsuit Filed Against Seattle School District; Settlements Announced in Two Other Washington Cities," January 20, 1995.

27. American Civil Liberties Union, press release, "PA High Court Says Schools Free to Search Student Lockers," January 14, 1998.

28. *Vernonia School Dist. 47J* v. *Acton*, 515 U.S. 646, 683-84 (1995).

29. Ibid.

30. Ibid., at 662.

31. Ibid.

32. *Todd* v. *Rush County Schools*, 133 F.3d 984 (7th Cir. 1998).

33. American Civil Liberties Union, press release, "Miami High School Students to Face Random Drug Tests," January 2, 1998.

34. *Willis* v. *Anderson Community School Corporation*, 158 F.3d 415, 422 (7th Cir. 1998).

35. "School Drug Tests Testing the Courts," *ABA Journal*, December 1998, p. 33.

Chapter 5. Freedom of Expression

1. *Tinker* v. *Des Moines Independent Community School District*, 393 U.S. 503 (1969).

2. Ibid., at 506.

3. Ibid., at 508.

4. *Bethel School District 403* v. *Fraser*, 478 U.S. 675, 687 (1986).

5. Ibid., at 683–684.

6. Ibid., at 682.

7. Ibid., at 681.

8. *Hazelwood School District* v. *Kuhlmeier*, 484 U.S. 260 (1988).

9. Ibid., at 271–272.

10. Ibid., at 271.

11. Michael Simpson, "How Free Is the Student Press?" *NEA Today*, November 1992, p. 25.

12. Ibid.

13. Student Press Law Center, November 9, 1999 <http://www.splc.org> (November 10, 1999).

14. American Civil Liberties Union, press release, "ACLU Wins Dismissal in Case of Fifteen-Year-Old Prosecuted for Underground Newspaper in Colorado," July 27, 1998; see also *Burch* v. *Barker*, 651 F. Supp. 1149 (W.D. Wash. 1987).

15. *Muller* v. *Jefferson Lighthouse School*, No. 95–3384 (7th Cir., October 30, 1996).

16. *Settle* v. *Dickson County School Board*, 53 F.3d 152, 153 (6th Cir. 1995).

17. Ibid., at 154.

18. Ibid., at 155.

19. *Board of Education, Island Trees Union Free School District No. 26* v. *Pico*, 457 U.S. 853, 856–857 (1982).

20. Ibid., at 853.

21. Ibid., at 867–868.

22. Ibid., at 880.

23. *Monteiro* v. *Tempe Union High School District*, 158 F.3d 1022 (9th Cir. 1998).

24. George Jefferson, "Confederate Flag T-shirts Get Two Students Suspended," *Lexington Herald-Leader*, September 18, 1997, <http://www.kentuckyconnect.com/heraldleader/news/091897/fn33con.html> (August 23, 1999).

25. American Civil Liberties Union, "ACLU Clients— Jeff and Jon Pyle," April 21, 1999, <http://www.aclu.org/court/clients/pyles.html> (August 23, 1999).

26. *Pyle* v. *School Committee of South Hadley*, 667 N.E.2d 869 (Mass. 1996).

27. Howard Pankratz, "Students Lose Kente-Cloth Fight," *Denver Post*, May 20, 1998, p. A1.

28. Paige Price, "Albuquerque Schools Bar Native Students' Traditional Attire at Graduation," Knight-Ridder/ Tribune Business News, April 7, 1997, p. 407B0930.

29. "Will School Uniforms Help Curb Student Violence," *Jet*, April 1, 1996, p. 12.

30. Said Deep, "Court Upholds School District on Dress Code," *Detroit News*, August 31, 1994, p. B1.

31. Deborah Tedford, "Students Win Rosary Case," *Houston Chronicle*, September 4, 1997, p. A25.

32. Andrea Atkins and Jeremy Schlosberg, "Dressed to Learn: Are Schools Better . . . When Kids Are in Uniform?" *Better Homes & Gardens*, August 1996, p. 42.

33. "Will School Uniforms Help Curb Student Violence," p. 12.

34. Lorraine Dusky, "At Summer's End, School Uniforms Put Focus on Learning," *USA Today*, September 1, 1998, p. 13A; Jacques Steinberg, "Head of Board of Education Offers Plan to Require School Uniforms," *The New York Times*, February 10, 1998, p. B1.

35. "Will School Uniforms Help Curb Student Violence," p. 12.

36. Telephone interview with Andy Brummé, staff attorney for ACLU of South Carolina, November 12, 1999; American Civil Liberties Union, press release, "Parents Sue SC School Over Uniform Policy," August 21, 1998.

Chapter 6. Going Online

1. *Reno v. American Civil Liberties Union*, 521 U.S. 844, 849 (1997).

2. Ibid., at 850.

3. Malcolm Maclachlan, "Digital Kids Result in Worried Parents," *TechWeb News*, June 24, 1998, <http://www.techweb.com/wire/story/TWB19980624S0019> (August 23, 1999).

4. Bruce Taylor, "Keep Libraries Porn-Free," *USA Today*, December 3, 1998, p. 24A.

5. *Reno v. American Civil Liberties Union*, at 861.

6. Ibid., at 844.

7. Ibid., at 875.

8. Linda Greenhouse, "Obscene E-mail," *The New York Times*, April 20, 1999, p. A16(N); Elinor Mills, "Supreme Court Upholds 'Annoying' CDA Provision," *CNN Interactive*, April 21, 1999, <http://cnn.com/TECH/computing/9904/21/annoy.idg/index.html> (August 23, 1999).

9. "Congress Passes Internet Child-Protection Measures," *American Libraries*, November 1998, p. 16.

10. American Civil Liberties Union, press release, "ACLU v. Reno Round 2: Update," November 19, 1998.

11. For example, S1619 and HR3177, both introduced during 1997–1998.

12. American Civil Liberties Union, "Congress Tries to Force Use of Clumsy Filtering Software," <http://www.aclu.org/action/jjfiltering106.html> (August 23, 1999).

13. "Peacefire," 1999, <http://www.peacefire.org> (November 10, 1999).

14. American Civil Liberties Union, press release, "ACLU Defends CA Library Against Parent Seeking to Compel Internet Censorship," July 10, 1998.

15. Jennifer Lenhart, "Lawsuit Challenges Internet Restrictions at Loudoun Libraries," *Washington Post*, December 23, 1997, p. B1.

16. American Civil Liberties Union, press release, "Virginia Court Says Internet Blocking for Adult Library Users Is Unconstitutional," November 23, 1998; "Today's Debate: Libraries and the Internet," *USA Today*, December 3, 1998, p. 24A.

17. Taylor, p. 24A.

18. American Civil Liberties Union, press release, "Court Upholds Livermore Library's Uncensored Internet Access Policy," January 14, 1999.

19. Cuyahoga County Public Library, "Especially for Parents: A Guide to the Internet," brochure, April 1997.

20. Kim Carter, "How to Teach Students the Rules of the Online Road," *Technology & Learning*, March 1998, p. 18.

21. Tamar Lewin, "Schools Challenge Students' Internet Talk," *The New York Times*, March 8, 1998, §1, p. 16.

22. Ibid.

23. Terry McManus, "Internet Raises New Rights Issues for Students," *Chicago Tribune*, April 21, 1998, §5, p. 1.

24. Mark Rollenhagen, "Judge Blocks Pupil's Suspension for Criticizing Teacher on Web," *Cleveland Plain Dealer*, March 19, 1998, p. 1A.

25. McManus, §5, p. 4.

26. Lewin, §1, p. 16.

27. American Civil Liberties Union, press release, "ACLU Wins Victory for Student Suspended Over Website Posting," December 28, 1998.

28. Ibid.

29. Lisa Bowman, "High School Suspends Net Access After Hack," ZDNN, March 25, 1998, <http://www.zdnet.com/zdnn/content/zdnn/292259.html> (August 23, 1999).

30. "Two Teens Plead Guilty to Hacking," *San Jose Mercury News*, July 30, 1998, p. 1C.

31. Telephone interview with Charles Palmer, IBM Global Security Analysis Laboratory, July 20, 1998.

32. Lewin, pp. 1–16.

33. Janet Tebben, "Schools Deal With Unease, Rumors," *Cleveland Plain Dealer*, May 10, 1999, p. 1B.

34. Telephone interview with Chris Link, Executive Director of ACLU of Ohio, November 12, 1999; American Civil Liberties Union, press release, "Ohio ACLU Defends Students Suspended Over Gothic-Themed Web Site," May 3, 1999.

Chapter 7. Curfews, Malls, Jobs, and Cars

1. Martin Pastrana, "Curfew: Collar or Life Vest?" *Cleveland Plain Dealer*, September 30, 1998, p. 1F.

2. John Allen, "U.S. Teens Face Rash of Get-Tough Actions as Nation's Fear Grows," *National Catholic Reporter*, January 10, 1997, p. 4.

3. American Civil Liberties Union, press release, "Survey: Youth Curfews on the Rise," December 1, 1997.

4. Kim Brown, "It's Best to Learn and Understand the Curfew Law(s)," *Cleveland Plain Dealer*, September 30, 1998, p. 2F.

5. "Bay Teens' Night of Fun in Cleveland Is Cut Short," *Sun Herald*, May 7, 1998, p. 3.

6. Ibid.

7. Evan Gohr, "Towns Turn Teens Into Pumpkins," *Insight on the News*, February 3, 1997, p. 40.

8. "Do Curfews Punish Innocent Teens?" *Current Events*, January 16, 1998, p. 3.

9. American Civil Liberties Union, press release, "New Jersey Council Stiffens Curfew Law," March 12, 1999.

10. Pastrana, p. 1F.

11. American Civil Liberties Union, press release, "Curfew Law Fails to Curb Violent Crime, Study Finds," February 17, 1998.

12. Gary Fields, "Study: Curfews Do Not Reduce Juvenile Crime," *USA Today*, June 10, 1998, p. 3A.

13. Joseph Santoro, "Police Chief Says Recent Curfew Study Not Grounded in Reality," *Nation's Cities Weekly*, August 31, 1998, p. 3.

14. Ibid.

15. American Civil Liberties Union, "Survey."

16. Santoro, p. 3.

17. Daniel Wood, "Curfew to Keep Youths off Streets Is Now off the Books," *Christian Science Monitor*, February 11, 1999, p. 2.

18. American Civil Liberties Union, press release, "Curfew Overturned in Washington State," June 2, 1997.

19. Ibid.

20. *Hutchins* v. *District of Columbia*, 144 F.3d 798 (D.C. Cir. 1998).

21. American Civil Liberties Union, press release, "Appeals Court Says D.C. Curfew Law Unconstitutional," May 22, 1998.

22. Alexandra Varney McDonald, "Major Bummer for Minors," *ABA Journal*, October 1999, p. 33.

23. *Schleifer* v. *City of Charlottesville*, 159 F.3d 843 (4th Cir. 1998).

24. Ibid., at 855.

25. Mall of America, "Parental Escort Policy," 1999, <http://www.mallofamerica.com/about/parental.htm> (November 10, 1999).

26. "Attention, Teenage Shoppers," *U.S. News & World Report*, October 7, 1996, p. 14.

27. Jean Palmieri, "Mall of America Mauled by Young Men's Merchants," *Daily News Record*, October 2, 1996, p. 1; Maureen Bausch, "Safety Is Our Top Priority," *USA Today*, September 10, 1996, p. A12.

28. Karl Vick, "Mall and Order in Minnesota," *Washington Post*, September 18, 1996, p. A1.

29. Robyn Meredith, "Big Mall's Curfew Raises Questions of Rights and Bias," *The New York Times*, September 4, 1996, pp. A1, B9.

30. Peggy Chisolm, "All of America Eyes Mall of America," *Daily News Record*, October 8, 1996, p. 1.

31. Telephone interview with Wendy Williams, June 7, 1999.

32. Mall of America, "Parental Escort Policy."

33. Ibid.

34. "Wired to Spend," *WWD*, February 19, 1998, p. S4.

35. Ibid.

36. Joseph M. Hawes, *The Children's Rights Movement: A History of Advocacy and Protection* (Boston: Twayne Publishers, 1991), pp. 48–49.

37. Fair Labor Standards Act, 29 United States Code, §201 et seq.

38. Ibid.

39. Ibid.

40. "Wired to Spend."

41. Ron Nixon, "Caution: Children at Work," *The Progressive*, August 1996, p. 30.

42. Ibid.

43. Ron Chepesick, "Peonage for Peach Pickers," *The Progressive*, December 1992, p. 22.

44. "Harvesting Heartache," *Occupational Hazards*, November 1995, p. 25.

45. Ibid.

46. Daniel Sutherland and Martha Hamilton, "Food Lion to Settle Claim It Violated U.S. Labor Law," *Washington Post*, August 4, 1993, p. A3.

47. James Warren, "White House Swings at Labor Law Curveball," *Chicago Tribune*, March 29, 1994, p. 1-1.

48. Deborah L. Forman, *Every Parent's Guide to the Law* (Orlando, Fla.: Harcourt Brace & Co., 1998), pp. 148–149.

49. "Independence Day: Macaulay Culkin Splits, Financially, From His Folks," *People Weekly*, March 17, 1997, p. 111.

50. "Wired to Spend."

51. Ibid.

52. Matthew Klein, "Teen Green," *American Demographics*, February 1998, p. 39.

53. Forman, pp. 145–147.

54. K. M. Kowalski, "The Dangers of Alcohol," *Current Health 2*, February 1998, p. 6.

Chapter 8. In Court

1. Joseph M. Hawes, *The Children's Rights Movement: A History of Advocacy and Protection* (Boston: Twayne Publishers, 1991), pp. 4–7.

2. Michael Brown, "Juvenile Offenders: Should They Be Tried in Adult Courts?" *USA Today Magazine*, January 1998, p. 52.

3. Hawes, p. 33.

4. Christopher Manfredi, *The Supreme Court and Juvenile Justice* (Lawrence: University of Kansas Press, 1998), pp. 86–87.

5. *In re Gault*, 387 U.S. 1, 28 (1967).

6. Fred Graham, "High Court Rules Adult Code Holds in Juvenile Trials," *The New York Times*, May 16, 1967, pp. 1, 36.

7. *In re Gault*, at 28.

8. *In re Winship*, 397 U.S. 358 (1970).

9. Manfredi, p. 134.

10. Ibid., pp. 134–135.

11. *In re Winship*, at 358.

12. *Johnson* v. *Upchurch*, CIV-86-195-TUC-RMB (D. Ariz., filed 1986).

13. David Lambert, "*Johnson* v. *Upchurch* Victory Brings Big Reforms in Arizona Juvenile Institutions," *Youth Law News*, March/April 1993, p. 2.

14. National Center for Youth Law, "Litigation Docket," June 8, 1999, <http://www.youthlaw.org/docket.htm> (November 10, 1999).

15. Gary Fields, "Courts Designed to Stop Teens at 'One Mistake,'" *USA Today*, June 7, 1999, p. 21A.

16. Ibid.

17. Tracy Godwin, "Teen Courts: Empowering Youth in Community Prevention and Intervention Efforts," *APPA Perspectives*, Winter 1996, p. 20; "Courts Designed to Stop Teens at 'One Mistake'."

18. Telephone interview with Lolita Junk, Knox County Teen Court Coordinator, November 13, 1998.

19. Ibid.

20. T. Trent Gegax, "A Search for Answers in a Wounded Town," *Newsweek*, April 13, 1998, p. 36.

21. Rick Bragg, "Arkansas Boys Who Killed 5 Are Sentenced," *The New York Times*, August 12, 1998, p. A1.

22. Brown, p. 52.

23. "Sixteen-Year-Old Boy Charged as Adult in Murder of Boy Over a Quarter," *Jet*, August 21, 1995, p. 37.

24. Julianne Malveaux, "Youth Crime Act Will Hurt More Than Help," *USA Today*, June 5, 1998, p. 13A.

25. Shannon Tangoman, "Jury Is Seated in Trial for School Shooting Spree," *USA Today*, June 10, 1998, p. 3A.

26. Carmine Sarracino, "Juvenile Predators, Adult Victims," *Insight on the News*, May 20, 1996, p. 28.

Glossary

censorship—Content-based restrictions on what one may say or write.

confidentiality—Trust that personal information will be kept secret.

consent—Permission; in a medical context, the agreement to allow a health-care provider to treat a condition.

consent decree—A voluntary agreement between two parties in a dispute.

corporal punishment—Physical punishment, such as spanking, swats, or hitting.

curfew—Law that makes it a crime for a person to be out on the streets under specified conditions.

custody—Duty to keep and provide a home for a minor, coupled with authority to make decisions affecting the minor.

deem—To make a legal assumption.

defer—To give a particular person's opinion greater weight, such as a parent who is presumed to have a child's best interests at heart.

delinquent—A child or teen who violates a criminal law.

discrimination—Differential treatment based on a characteristic such as race, gender, or age.

due process—Legal procedures designed to ensure fair hearings and trials.

emancipation—The process by which a teen under age eighteen is deemed or declared a legal adult.

expulsion—Permanent removal of a student from school.

Internet—A worldwide computer network used for research, entertainment, commerce, and communications.

lawsuit—Court proceeding to settle a legal dispute.

luxury—Something beyond basic needs that is not essential for survival.

mature minor—Term used in some states for a teen who may not be emancipated but who is allowed to give informed consent for medical treatment.

minor—A person who has not yet reached the age where he or she becomes a legal adult; in the United States, generally a person under age eighteen.

necessity—An item such as food, clothing, or shelter that is required for a person's survival and well-being.

permanent record—Official school files kept about a student, including transcript of classes and grades, records of disciplinary actions, recommendations, family data, and other comments or notes recorded by teachers or school personnel.

probation—Period when a person remains under court supervision following release from custody or suspension of a jail sentence.

prosecute—To press criminal charges against a person.

rehabilitate—To train a person to substitute socially acceptable behavior for illegal conduct.

sexual harassment—Behavior that demeans a person because of gender or demands sexual favors in return for beneficial treatment.

sue—File a lawsuit.

suspension—Temporary exclusion of a student from school.

Further Reading

Cary, Eve, et al. *The Rights of Students*. New York: Puffin Books, 1997.

Edmonds, Beverly, and William Fernekes. *Children's Rights: A Reference Handbook*. Santa Barbara, Calif.: ABC-CLIO, Inc., 1996.

Fischer, Louis, and Gail Paulus Sorensen. *School Law for Counselors, Psychologists, and Social Workers*. 3rd ed. White Plains, N. Y.: Longman Publishers, 1996.

Fischer, Louis, et al. *Teachers and the Law*. 4th ed. White Plains, N. Y.: Longman Publishers, 1995.

Forman, Deborah L. *Every Parent's Guide to the Law*. Orlando, Fla.: Harcourt Brace & Co., 1998.

Gold, Susan. *In re Gault (1967): Juvenile Justice*. New York: Twenty-First Century Books, 1995.

Hempelman, Kathleen. *Teen Legal Rights: A Guide for the '90's*. Westport, Conn.: Greenwood Press, 1994.

Jasper, Margaret. *Juvenile Justice and Children's Law*. Dobbs Ferry, N. Y.: Oceana Publications, 1994.

Lane, Robert Wheeler. *Beyond the Schoolhouse Gate: Free Speech and the Inculcation of Values*. Philadelphia: Temple University Press, 1995.

Manfredi, Christopher. *The Supreme Court and Juvenile Justice*. Lawrence: University of Kansas Press, 1998.

Index